Federal Housing Subsidies: How Are They Working?

Real Estate Research Corporation is a professional consulting organization specializing in economic and real estate analysis for business, government and investors. Since its founding in 1931, RERC has focused exclusively on research and social and organizational analysis. The company is headquartered in Chicago and has eleven regional offices across the country.

Federal Housing Subsidies: How Are They Working?

Anthony Downs
Real Estate Research Corporation

This study was jointly sponsored by:

National Association of Home Builders
National Association of Mutual Savings Banks
United States Savings and Loan League

Lexington Books
D.C. Heath and Company
Lexington, Massachusetts
Toronto   London

Library of Congress Cataloging in Publication Data

Real Estate Research Corporation.
   Federal housing subsidies.

   Bibliography: p.
   1. Housing- United States- Finance. 2. Subsidies- United States.
   I. Downs, Anthony. II. Title.
HD7392.R36   301.5'4   73-1608
ISBN 0-669-86777-2

Published simultanously in Canada.

Printed in the United States of America.

International Standard Book Number: 0-669-86777-2

Library of Congress Catalog Card Number: 73-1608

Table of Contents

List of Tables

List of Charts

Preface

Nature of the Assignment

The purpose of this study was to conduct a factually accurate and objective analysis of existing and proposed federal housing subsidies. In order to achieve this general goal, the study was intended to provide answers to the following specific questions:

1. What are the *basic objectives* of federal government housing subsidies or other forms of government housing assistance?
2. What specific *criteria of desirability* should be used to help evaluate the relative merits of various forms of housing subsidies or other forms of government assistance, in addition to determining the degree to which they achieve their basic objectives?
3. What was the *basic intent of Congress* in establishing the Section 235 and Section 236 housing subsidy programs in the Housing and Urban Development Act of 1968? How well have those programs, as subsequently carried out, fulfilled that intent?
4. What *specific difficulties or problems* have emerged from practical experience with the Section 235 and Section 236 programs—considered separately—that result from their particular structure or operation, in contrast to problems or difficulties that would be associated with any high volume subsidy program? How are those specific problems and difficulties different in the new construction, existing, and rehabilitation portions of the Section 235 and Section 236 programs? How might those problems and difficulties be remedied without destroying the basic viability or effectiveness of these programs?
5. What *alternative forms of subsidy* might be developed to meet the objectives of housing subsidies, other than interest rate subsidies? What would be the likely costs, effectiveness, advantages, and disadvantages of each such alternative? How effectively would each major form of subsidy (including interest rate subsidies) achieve each of the basic objectives of housing subsidy programs? And how effectively would it meet the other criteria of desirability?
6. What should be the *role of new housing unit production* in the nation's strategy for meeting its housing needs? How does that role compare with the proper roles for other forms of housing or housing-related assistance that do not stress new production?

Answering the above questions has proved to be an extraordinarily difficult and complex task. However, we have tried to present the answers we have found in as brief and easily comprehensible a manner as possible. Nonetheless, we have had to include enough information and analysis to avoid the all-too-common errors caused by grossly oversimplified approaches to evaluating housing subsidies.

Method of Analysis

Most of the findings in the study have been based upon a thorough analysis of existing legislation, official records, and other literature concerning housing subsidies, rather than original research. However, we also conducted the following original research projects as a basis for our findings:

1. We visited HUD regional offices in seven cities, interviewed several officials connected with housing subsidies in each office, inspected specific subsidized housing projects in each area, and talked to private developers of some of those projects. The cities were Minneapolis, Milwaukee, St. Louis, Chicago, Detroit, Atlanta, and Des Moines.
2. We constructed computerized models of specific forms of housing subsidies and tested relationships between subsidy costs and rent reductions under different assumptions.
3. We submitted requests to the Office of the Deputy Under Secretary of the Department of Housing and Urban Development for information on housing subsidies that had not previously been gathered, and received many special tabulations in return.
4. We interviewed several developers and accountants connected with subsidized housing projects concerning their desirability as investments, and problems involved in carrying out such projects.

The result is what we believe is the most comprehensive overview of federal housing subsidies ever conducted. This book presents only a summary of the main findings of the analysis, since an exposition of the entire study would be too lengthy for convenient use by the busy people whose decisions are most influential in this field.

Objectivity of the Analysis and Conclusions

This study has been conducted in as objective and impartial a manner as possible. We undertook the assignment only on condition that we would express the facts as we saw them, regardless of their impacts upon public policies or upon the interests of any particular groups—including those organizations that funded the study. In almost all cases, the *quantitative data* used in this analysis represent the joint findings of Real Estate Research Corporation and the U.S. Department of Housing and Urban Development, and have been agreed upon as substantially accurate by both ourselves and HUD. However, all *conclusions and judgments* based upon these data represent the views of Real Estate Research Corporation alone, and do not necessarily reflect the views of HUD, any of our other clients, or the organizations who cooperated in making this study possible.

Acknowledgements

We are grateful to the Department of Housing and Urban Development, especially Deputy Under Secretary Charles Orlebeke and Gary Kopff, for outstanding cooperation in providing us with vital information. We are also grateful to the organizations that funded this study—the National Association of Home Builders, the United States Savings and Loan League, and the National Association of Mutual Savings Banks—for their excellent cooperation. We especially appreciate their faithfully honoring their pledge to give us complete freedom to conduct the study in the manner we believed would most clearly and impartially present the truth about this complex subject.

Three people associated with the National Association of Home Builders deserve our special thanks. Dr. Nathaniel H. Rogg, Executive Vice President, strongly supported the concept of this study, contributed his thoughts and ideas, and endorsed RERC's independence in presenting the results of the analysis. As head of the executive committee that worked with us on this assignment, Marvin S. Gilman of Leon N. Weiner and Associates exhibited understanding about the complexity of the issues and provided thoughtful criticism of our analyses. Peter E. Kaplan, now with Brownstein, Zeidman and Schomer, offered valuable criticism and served as liaison between RERC and the sponsors.

Many staff members of Real Estate Research Corporation assisted in the research and analyses required to reach the conclusions and recommendations presented in this book. The specialized analytical projects performed by the following persons were integral to completion of the study: Alfred K. Eckersberg, Ellen A. Jacknain, M. Leanne Lachman, Sedgwick Mead, Jr., Audrey Burkes, Frances Sontag, and Roderick E. MacIver.

1

The Basic Nature of Housing Subsidies, Their Objectives, and Housing Needs

Nature of Housing Subsidies

1. Housing subsidies are any forms of economic assistance provided to the producers or consumers of housing, at the expense of others in the economy, in order to lower the price or costs of housing, or factors related to it, so as to encourage the output, supply, and use of decent quality housing by American households.[1]

2. Housing subsidies encompass a bewildering variety of specific devices, many of which do not show up in the federal budget. There are two basic types of housing subsidies:
   - *Direct* housing subsidies have been explicitly adopted by Congress to serve the objectives stated below. They involve clear payments to the producers or consumers of housing, and appear in the federal budget.
   - *Indirect* housing subsidies consist mainly of federal income tax savings from certain tax regulations related to housing. Some indirect subsidies are "accidental" results of regulations not explicitly adopted to serve the objectives stated below. Indirect subsidies do *not* appear in the federal budget, and are therefore neither clearly visible nor easily measurable. Nevertheless, they are just as real and significant as direct subsidies.

Objectives of Housing Subsidies

1. Federal housing subsidies are major instruments useful in achieving the "national housing goal . . . of a decent home and a suitable living environment for every American family," as stated by Congress in the Housing Act of 1949 and reaffirmed in the Housing and Urban Development Act of 1968.[2]

2. Legislation creating housing subsidies has been designed to serve thirteen specific objectives. Those that appear to be *primary* are as follows: [3]
   - Providing housing assistance to low-income households by enabling such households now living in substandard quality housing to occupy decent units, and by aiding such households who now pay inordinately high fractions of their incomes to live in decent units.

- 2 • Providing housing assistance to moderate-income households in the same ways described above.
- 3 • Providing housing assistance to numerous specific groups in the same manner as described above. These groups include the elderly, Indians, persons displaced by government action, disabled veterans, etc.
- 4 • Encouraging homeownership among households, regardless of their incomes.
- 5 • Stimulating the economy by increasing activity in the housing industry.
- 6 • Increasing the total available supply of decent quality dwelling units.
- 7 • Improving the quality of deteriorated neighborhoods.

3. Objectives of housing subsidies that appear *secondary*, but still important, are as follows:

- 8 • Providing housing assistance to colleges.
- 9 • Stabilizing the annual output of the housing industry at a high level.
- 10 • Encouraging housing innovations that improve design, reduce costs, and improve quality.
- 11 • Creating opportunities for employment, entrepreneurship, and training among residents of low-income areas.
- 12 • Encouraging maximum feasible participation of private enterprise and capital in meeting housing needs.
- 13 • Achieving greater spatial dispersion of low- and moderate-income housing outside areas of concentrated poverty. (This objective is not derived from congressional legislation.)

4. Housing subsidies should also conform to certain general criteria of desirability for federal spending programs, insofar as possible. These criteria are not formally established in legislation, but are widely recognized in administrative practice and in analyses of subsidy programs. They are shown in chart 4.1 later in the book.

5. The specific quantitative housing production goal set forth in the Housing and Urban Development Act of 1968 is creation of 26 million new or rehabilitated decent quality housing units from 1968 to 1978, including six million made available to low- and moderate-income households by various subsidies.

Need for Housing Subsidies to Accomplish These Objectives

1. Needs for housing subsidies arise from three fundamental conditions in the United States:
   - *Poverty* causes millions of households to have incomes so low that they can only afford relatively small annual payments for housing.
   - *Relatively high quality standards* legally required for newly built hous-

ing prevent the creation of any *new* units inexpensive enough for poor households to occupy without financial assistance.

• *Neighborhood linkage effects* cause the quality of life of each household to be affected by the behavior of other households around it, and therefore create a desire among middle-income and upper-income households to exclude poorer households from their neighborhoods.

The first and third conditions are found in all nations, but the second is relatively unique to the United States.

2. These three fundamental conditions are combined in the basic "trickle- *filtering* down" urban development process that dominates urban growth in the United States. High quality new housing units are constructed mainly on the periphery of built-up urban areas. They are occupied by households in the upper half of the income distribution, since they are too expensive for low- and moderate-income households. As these units become older, they are occupied by households with relatively lower and lower incomes. Eventually, the once new units "trickle down" to households too poor to maintain them; then they deteriorate rapidly. Universal laws against low quality housing units are rigorously enforced in new-growth areas, but virtually ignored in older, more central areas where poor households live. Consequently, the urban poor cannot live in any new-growth areas or most well-kept older areas because of legally created high costs there. So they are concentrated in areas of low-quality housing. Such concentration multiplies and reinforces the normal problems associated with poverty. This creates extremely undesirable neighborhood environments, from which most nonpoor households depart if they can.

The entire process results in excellent housing and neighborhoods for the wealthy; good housing and neighborhoods for the middle class; and poor housing (in relation to its cost) and disastrous neighborhoods for the very poor. *Most of the nation's urban "housing problems" result directly from a combination of poverty per se and the way this process compels the poorest households to bear the social costs of creating desirable neighborhood environments for the upper two-thirds of the income distribution* (which contains a clear majority of Americans).

3. A relatively high proportion of the nation's inadequate housing is located in rural areas. They contained 46 percent of all substandard housing in 1966, though only about 27 percent of the population lived in such areas. [4] Rural housing needs also arise mainly from poverty, but they have a different character from urban housing needs. Housing is priced much lower in rural than in urban areas. Inadequate plumbing is the single biggest cause of physical substandardness in rural housing. Also, rural housing deficiencies arise in a dynamic setting marked by constantly declining population, weak legal controls on the quality of new construction, scattered sites for individual units, and a relatively disorganized housing construction industry. Hence,

rural housing needs are less involved with neighborhood linkage effects and economic segregation than urban housing needs.

Kinds of Housing Needs Arising from These Causes

1. The nation's housing deficiencies have given rise to two different conceptions of "housing needs," as follows:
   - *Financial housing needs* arise because many households have a "gap" between the amount they could devote to housing if they spent "normal" percentages of their incomes on it, and the actual cost of decent quality housing units (those meeting socially defined minimum standards). For example, if a four-person household has an annual income of $3,000, it can pay only $750 for housing if it spends the "normal" 25 percent on shelter. If a decent quality unit costs $1,200 per year to occupy, this household has a "gap" of $450 per year ($1,200 minus $750). One way to help reduce or eliminate this gap is with a subsidy that reduces the effective cost of occupancy for this household, or raises its income, or both.[5]
   - *Physical housing needs* arise when there are not enough decent quality housing units in existence, and at proper locations, so that every household can occupy one, regardless of how much it pays to do so. The private market alone never eliminates physical housing needs, mainly because many poor households cannot afford to occupy units meeting legally required quality standards. Housing subsidies can be used to stimulate greater housing output than the private market would produce alone, thereby helping to meet these needs. Forecasts of *future* physical needs must take into account requirements of additional units to accommodate future population growth and future removal of decent units from the inventory, as well as the replacement of substandard quality units.'
2. These two concepts of "housing needs" are very different, and have different policy implications. Specifically:
   - *Financial housing needs result mainly from poverty,* rather than the physical condition of the housing inventory. Most households with financial housing needs actually occupy decent quality dwelling units, but pay high fractions of their incomes to do so. Unpublished 1970 Census data indicate that 85 percent of all "poverty households" occupied housing that did not lack "complete, private plumbing." Yet 81 percent of the families with incomes below $5,000 paid over 25 percent of their gross incomes for gross rent and 62 percent paid over 35 percent of their incomes for rent.[6] Hence, curing financial housing needs mainly requires raising the incomes of poor households, either directly through

income maintenance, or indirectly through housing allowances or other subsidies.

- *Physical housing needs* refer only to housing unit quality, not the incomes of the occupants. Curing physical housing needs is mainly a matter of producing additional decent quality dwelling units, and eliminating or improving existing substandard quality units. However, since the private market alone will not produce enough new units to achieve these goals, some forms of construction-oriented subsidies are necessary to do so.

3. The nation's official housing production goal of 26 million newly created units from 1968 to 1978 is based almost exclusively upon the *physical housing needs* concept described above. It is true that the official target of six million newly created units for low- and moderate-income households is derived in part from the *financial housing needs* concept. Yet this target for subsidized units is *not* designed to meet all financial housing needs, but only enough of those needs to make it possible to meet physical housing needs completely by 1978. Hence, if the national housing goals were fulfilled, there would be enough standard quality housing units for every American household as of 1978. But many poor households would still be paying relatively high fractions of their incomes to occupy such units.

Notes

1. This definition is derived from the discussion of subsidies in general set forth in the Joint Economic Committee's staff study, *The Economics of Federal Subsidy Programs* (Washington, D.C., January 11, 1972), pp. 7–12.
2. Committee on Banking and Currency, U.S. House of Representatives, *Basic Laws and Authorities on Housing and Urban Development* (Washington, D.C., revised through January 31, 1971), p. 1.
3. These objectives are taken from various specific statutes as set forth in *Basic Laws and Authorities on Housing and Urban Development.*
4. Charles L. Schultze, Edward R. Fried, Alice M. Rivlin, and Nancy H. Teeters, *Setting National Priorities: The 1972 Budget* (Washington, D.C., 1971(1), p. 291. It should be noted that the Census Bureau definition of "substandard" is limited and focuses on plumbing facilities. It does not consider overcrowding; it does not take into consideration the proportion of income spent on housing; it does not reflect adequacy of heating equipment.
5. These figures correspond roughly to some used by The Urban Institute in computations concerning a national housing allowance. See John D. Heinberg, *The Transfer Cost of a Housing Allowance: Conceptual Issues and Benefit Patterns* (Washington, D.C., May 1971).
6. Letter to Real Estate Research Corporation from Office of the Deputy Under Secretary, Department of Housing and Urban Development, August 16, 1972.

2

The Size of Housing Subsidies, and
the Number of Housing Units
They Have Created

Present Size of Federal Housing Subsidies

1. In fiscal 1970, federal housing subsidies cost about $8.4 billion, although less than $2.0 billion of that total appeared in the federal budget. These housing subsidies comprised about 13 percent of all federal subsidies in that year, as computed by the Joint Economic Committee staff. Federal housing subsidies exceeded all other forms of federal subsidies in total amount except those for general commerce plus community development, and those for medical care.[1]

2. The biggest housing subsidies resulted from deductibility of mortgage interest and property taxes from taxable income by homeowner-occupants, which saved them $5.4 billion in taxes in fiscal 1970 and $5.7 billion in fiscal 1971. These subsidies provide far larger benefits per household to high-income households than to either middle-income, moderate-income, or low-income households.[2]

   • In 1966, 69 percent of the tax savings that formed these subsidies were received by households with annual incomes of over $10,000, and 90 percent by households with incomes of over $7,000. The median family income in that year was $7,436. Hence, the vast majority of these subsidies went to the upper half of the income distribution. Households with incomes of under $3,000 received less than one percent of these subsidies.[3]

3. Additional subsidies, in the form of tax deductions, are available to investors in some forms of housing. The Treasury Department reports a total subsidy of $500 million in calendar year 1971 to owners of rental housing who used accelerated instead of straight-line depreciation. (Of this total, $300 million were claimed by corporations and $200 million by individuals.) Another $25 million in deductions were claimed by corporations ($10 million) and individuals ($15 million) who rehabilitated existing housing units for low-income occupancy and were entitled to a five-year write-off of costs.[4]

4. A related form of housing assistance not technically a subsidy is the housing portion of public assistance payments, which totaled approximately $3.0 billion in 1970. About half was federally funded. This aid goes almost entirely to very low-income households, but in many cases does not provide them with decent quality units.[5]

7

5. Federal housing subsidies totaled an amount slightly under one percent of gross national product in fiscal 1970, or just about one percent if welfare rent payments are included.
6. Complete tabulations of federal housing subsidy costs for fiscal 1971 and 1972 are not available. However, they are certainly larger than the $8.4 billion for fiscal 1970. We estimate they totaled about $8.6 billion in fiscal 1971 and slightly more than that in fiscal 1972.

Size of Direct Federal Budget Outlays for Housing

1. Budget outlays for subsidized housing programs totaled $1.46 billion in fiscal 1971, which was slightly above the 1970 figure of $1.40 billion. In fiscal 1972, the estimated outlay for subsidized housing is $1.82 billion, and the 1973 estimate is $2.13 billion.[6]
2. The Department of Housing and Urban Development alone made budget outlays of $734 million for housing subsidies in fiscal 1971, and estimates that such outlays will total $1.110 billion in fiscal 1972 and $1.771 billion in fiscal 1973. This represents an increase of 141 percent in two years. The relation of these outlays to HUD's total budget is shown in table 2-1.

Number of Subsidized Housing Units Created

1. Because all homeowner-occupants who do not use the standardized deduction in computing their federal income tax receive an indirect housing subsidy, and because this is by far the largest housing subsidy, it would almost be fair to conclude that all owner-occupied housing units have been at least partially subsidized. In 1970, there were 39.9 million owner-occupied housing units in the United States. They comprised 62.9 percent of all occupied units. The number of such units rose 16.3 million from 1950 to 1970. It is impossible to determine the extent to which homeownership, as opposed to rental, has been encouraged by this major housing subsidy. However, its impact has undoubtedly been very significant.[7]
2. Direct federal housing subsidies have been responsible for the creation of 2.3 million housing units from 1935 through 1971 (excluding temporary war housing built during World War II). This is an annual average of 61,655 over 37 years.[8]
3. Production of directly subsidized units has remarkably accelerated since 1967, as shown in table 2-2.

Thus, over half of all the directly subsidized units ever built in the United States were constructed from 1968 through 1971. The annual rate of sub-

Table 2-1

Housing Subsidy Payments in Relation to HUD's Overall Budget, 1971–1973 (Billions of Dollars)

Item	Fiscal 1971 (Actual)	Fiscal 1972 (Estimated)	Fiscal 1973 (Estimated)
HUD *Gross* Budget Outlays	$6.2	$7.3	$8.7
HUD *Net* Budget Outlays*	2.890	3.652	4.214
Housing Subsidy Outlays	0.734	1.110	1.771
Housing Subsidy Outlays as Percentage of *Net* Budget Outlays	25.3%	30.4%	42.0%

*Net budget outlays are equal to gross budget outlays, less proceeds from sales of financial assets (i.e., mortgage fees and premiums on insured mortgages, which usually exceed insurance claims).

Source: Subcommittee of Committee on Appropriations, House of Representatives, 92nd Congress 2nd Session, *HUD-Space-Science-Veterans Appropriations for 1973, Hearings, Part 3*, pp. 6, 133.

Table 2-2

Creation of Directly Subsidized Housing Units, 1935–1971

Calendar Year Period	Total Directly Subsidized Units Created	Number of Years	Annual Average Number Created
1935–1949	200,754	15	13,384
1950–1959	409,057	10	40,906
1960–1967	446,675	8	55,834
1968–1971	1,224,760	4	306,190

Source: U.S. Department of Housing and Urban Development, Division of Research and Statistics.

sidized housing production in those four years averaged 5.5 times that in the early 1960s, and 7.5 times that in the 1950s.[9]

Subsidized Housing as a Proportion of Total Housing Production

1. Before 1966, direct housing subsidies generated very small shares of total conventional housing production each year—never exceeding 4.8 percent, and averaging less than that. Total subsidized and nonsubsidized housing production is shown for both conventional units and mobile homes in table 2-4 for the period 1950 through March 1972.[10]

2.   From 1966 onward, the share of subsidized units in total conventional hous-
     ing production rose rapidly, as indicated in table 2–3.

Table 2–3
Directly Subsidized Units as a Proportion of Total Housing Production,
1966–1971

		Percentage of Total Housing Production Generated by Direct Federal Subsidies	
Calendar Year	Number of Directly Subsidized Units Started	Conventional Units Only in Total	Mobile Homes Included in Total
1966	71,632	6.0%	5.1%
1967	91,433	6.9%	5.9%
1968	163,360	10.6%	8.8%
1969	196,930	13.1%	10.3%
1970	430,990	29.4%	23.1%
1971	433,480	20.8%	16.8%

Source: Table 2–4.

3.   From 1968 through 1971, directly subsidized housing units have accounted
     for 18.6 percent of all conventionally built housing in the United States,
     and 14.9 percent of all new housing, including mobile homes. In 1970 and
     1971 combined, such subsidized units comprised one out of every four new
     conventional units, and one out of every five total new units. Preliminary
     evidence indicates they will comprise about one out of every six conven-
     tional units in 1972.

Number of Directly Subsidized Units by Program

1.   Detailed breakdowns of subsidized housing production by program for the
     calendar years 1968 through April 1972 are presented in tables 2–5 and
     2–6. The numbers of newly constructed and rehabilitated units are shown
     separately by year and by program. Table 2–7 summarizes the figures.[11]
2.   These figures do *not* include the subsidized occupancy of 172,330 *existing*
     decent quality units provided for by direct housing subsidies during the fis-
     cal years 1969 through 1971. Of this total, 57,270 units (33.2 percent) were
     subsidized under the Section 235 program; 67,360 units (39.1 percent)
     under Department of Agriculture programs; and 47,700 units (27.7 percent)
     under public housing programs. We have not included these existing units in
     our analysis of subsidized housing *production*, since subsidizing their occu-
     pancy did not add to the total housing supply. However, it did add 11.7 per-
     cent to the total number of newly built and rehabilitated subsidized units in
     the same four fiscal years.

Table 2–4

Annual Housing Starts by Type, 1950–1972

Calendar Year	Conventionally-Constructed Housing Starts*			Non-subsidized Starts	Mobile Homes	Total–All Housing Starts
	Total	Subsidized Starts**	Percentage Subsidized			
1950	1,951,648	43,648	2.2%	1,908,000	63,100	2,014,748
1951	1,491,207	71,207	4.8%	1,420,000	67,300	1,558,507
1952	1,504,520	58,520	3.9%	1,446,000	83,000	1,587,520
1953	1,438,372	35,483	2.5%	1,402,889	76,900	1,515,272
1954	1,550,445	18,638	1.2%	1,531,807	76,000	1,626,445
1955	1,645,715	18,751	1.1%	1,626,964	111,900	1,757,615
1956	1,345,739	20,739	1.5%	1,325,000	104,800	1,450,539
1957	1,221,647	46,647	3.8%	1,175,000	107,600	1,329,247
1958	1,375,588	61,588	4.5%	1,314,000	100,400	1,475,988
1959	1,528,836	33,836	2.2%	1,495,000	120,500	1,649,336
1960	1,272,137	42,087	3.3%	1,230,050	103,700	1,375,837
1961	1,365,000	36,162	2.6%	1,328,838	90,200	1,455,200
1962	1,492,400	38,815	2.6%	1,453,585	118,000	1,610,400
1963	1,642,000	47,829	2.9%	1,594,171	150,840	1,792,840
1964	1,561,000	55,117	3.5%	1,505,883	191,320	1,752,320
1965	1,509,600	63,600	4.2%	1,446,000	216,000	1,725,600
1966	1,195,900	71,632	6.0%	1,124,268	217,000	1,412,900
1967	1,321,817	91,433	6.9%	1,230,384	240,000	1,561,817
1968	1,545,500	163,360	10.6%	1,382,140	318,000	1,863,500
1969	1,499,920	196,930	13.1%	1,302,990	413,000	1,912,920
1970	1,466,759	430,990	29.4%	1,035,769	401,000	1,867,759
1971	2,084,500	433,480	20.8%	1,651,020	496,570	2,581,070
Jan.–Mar. 1972	509,300	75,673	14.9%	433,627	121,820	631,120

*Conventionally *constructed* housing starts can be financed with either VA- and FHA-insured mortgages or *conventional mortgages*.

**These totals do not include *existing* or *rehabilitated* units subsidized—only *newly built* units.

Sources: U.S. Department of Housing and Urban Development, Division of Research and Statistics; and Mobile Home Manufacturers Association.

3. We have provided detailed data for only 1968 to 1972 because:
   - Over half of all the directly subsidized units ever built were produced in these years.
   - The major subsidy programs now in use were created in 1968; hence, data concerning this period cover their entire lifetime, and are more current than data in earlier periods. Many programs more active in earlier periods are being phased out.
   - The vast majority of all subsidized units produced before 1968 were public housing units, partly because most other direct subsidy programs did not exist very long before 1968.

Table 2-5
Directly Subsidized Housing Production of New Units by Program, Calendar Years 1968–April 1972 (in numbers of housing units)

Programs	1968	1969	1970	1971	Jan.–April 1972	Total	Percentage of Subsidized Units	
							New Units Only	All Units
Section 235 (1-4 family)	637	28,127	116,073	140,728	41,486	327,051	24.9%	22.4%
Public Housing								
Conventional	42,240	27,598	30,536	18,022	3,146	121,542		
Turnkey	18,353	31,095	52,286	38,375	3,307	143,416		
Leased	7,600	8,368	16,044	11,634	2,116	45,762		
Total	68,193	67,061	98,866	68,031	8,569	310,720	23.6%	21.3%
Section 202 (for elderly)	6,440**	7,423	2,984	947	—	17,794	1.4%	1.2%
Rent Supplement (excluding those tied to Section 236)	16,720**	17,912	22,919	9,861	2,011	69,423	5.3%	4.7%
Section 221(d)(3)	45,403	33,439	16,544	5,659	222	101,267	7.7%	6.9%
Section 236	—	10,168	105,160	108,681	16,489	240,498	18.3%	16.5%
Uninsured State Projects	796	2,881	10,817	24,927	2,001	41,422	3.1%	2.8%
U.S. Department of Agriculture	27,170**	29,920**	57,630**	74,670**	19,824*	207,214	15.7%	14.2%
Total New Units	163,359	196,931	430,993	433,504	90,602	1,315,389	100.0%	90.0%

*Through March only.
**Rounded.
Source: U.S. Department of Housing and Urban Development.

Table 2-6
Directly Subsidized Housing Rehabilitations by Program, Calendar Years 1968–April 1972 (in numbers of housing units)

Rehabilitations	1968	1969	1970	1971	Jan.–April 1972	Total	Percentage of Subsidized Units Rehabilitated Units Only	All Units
1-4 Family								
Section 221(h)	744	1,897	615	55	—	3,311	2.3%	
Section 235(j)	—	55	1,253	1,524	117	2,949	2.0%	
Section 235(i)	—	—	238	588	230	1,056	0.7%	
Section 115/312	3,425	7,537	11,103	11,912	3,755	37,732	25.7%	
Total 1-4 Family–HUD	4,169	9,489	13,209	14,079	4,102	45,048	30.7%	3.1%
Multi-Family								
Public Housing–Turnkey, Leased	7,245	5,346	5,544	4,219	579	22,933	15.6%	
Section 221(d)(3)	5,602	3,862	1,555	423	75	11,517	7.9%	
Section 236	—	347	5,883	6,043	2,729	15,002	10.2%	
Rent Supplement (excluding those tied to Section 236)	180*	438	1,691	2,068	578	4,955	3.4%	
Section 202	160*	—	—	—	—	160	0.1%	
Section 115/312	—	—	570*	931	302	1,803	1.2%	
Total Multi-Family–HUD	13,187	9,993	15,240	13,684	4,263	56,370	38.5%	3.9%
U.S. Department of Agriculture	11,061	9,950*	11,644	10,280*	2,213	45,148	30.8%	3.1%
Total Units Rehabilitated	28,417	29,432	40,093	38,043	10,578	146,566	100.0%	10.0%

*Rounded.

Source: U.S. Department of Housing and Urban Development.

Table 2-7

Summary of Directly Subsidized Housing Production, Calendar Years 1968–
April 1972* (in numbers of housing units)

Type of Units	1968	1969	1970	1971	Jan.-April 1972	Total
Total New Construction	163,359	196,931	430,993	433,504	90,602	1,315,389
Total Rehabilitation	28,417	29,432	40,093	38,043	10,578	146,563
Total—All Directly Subsidized Units	191,776	226,363	471,086	471,547	101,180	1,461,952
Percentage of Total for Period, by Year	13.1%	15.5%	32.2%	32.3%	6.9%	100.0%
Annual Percentage of Total Subsidized Units						
New Starts	85.2%	87.0%	91.5%	91.9%	89.6%	90.0%
Rehabilitation	14.8%	13.0%	8.5%	8.1%	10.4%	10.0%

*These figures do *not* include the subsidized occupancy of 172,330 *existing* decent quality
housing units provided for by direct housing subsidies during the fiscal years 1969 through
1971. Nor do the figures include housing provided under programs of the Departments of
Defense and Interior.
Source: U.S. Department of Housing and Urban Development.

4.   The following significant conclusions can be drawn from these tables:
   - New construction has accounted for 90 percent of all housing units
     produced by direct subsidies in this period. This is somewhat larger than
     its planned share of 84 percent. Hence, rehabilitation is falling even fur-
     ther behind planned targets than new construction.
   - Among newly constructed units, the vast majority have been created in
     multi-family structures. However, the share of single-family structures
     is rising because of the rapid expansion of the Section 235 program.
     Multi-family units accounted for 70.5 percent of all HUD-subsidized
     new units during this period. This is equivalent to 59.1 percent of all
     new subsidized units (a breakdown of Department of Agriculture units
     by structure type was not available, but most are single-family homes).
     However, single-family units have risen from almost none in 1968 to
     over 45 percent of all newly built subsidized units in early 1972.
   - About two-thirds of the subsidized units constructed in this period are
     for moderate-income households, and about one-third for low-income
     households.[12] The number of low-income units can be estimated by
     adding up all public housing units, 20 percent of all Section 236 units,
     and all rent supplement units. This totals 415,841 units, or 28.5 percent

of all newly built subsidized units created in this period. This total may
be somewhat too high, because less than 20 percent of all Section 236
units have actually had rent supplements attached to them. However,
some Section 235 units have been occupied by low-income households;
so we assume these two sources of error approximately cancel.

★ The Section 235 and 236 programs are accounting for a rising share of
all newly built subsidized units, and contributed almost two-thirds of
all such units in the first four months of 1972. The proportions of all
newly built directly subsidized units in these two programs and in the
public housing program are shown in table 2-8.

Table 2-8
Percentage of All Newly Built Directly Subsidized Units in Key Programs, 1968–
April 1972

Calendar Year	Section 235	Section 236	Total 235 + 236	All Public Housing Programs	Other Programs
1968	0.4%	0.0%	0.4%	41.7%	57.9%
1969	14.3%	5.2%	19.5%	34.1%	46.4%
1970	26.9%	24.4%	51.3%	22.9%	25.8%
1971	32.5%	25.1%	57.6%	15.7%	26.7%
1972 (4 months)	45.8%	18.2%	64.0%	10.6%	25.4%

Source: U.S. Department of Housing and Urban Development.

- Public housing programs have contributed a steadily diminishing proportion of all new subsidized units since 1968, and a declining absolute
  number per year since reaching a peak in 1970.
- Consequently, the share of moderate-income units in total directly
  subsidized starts has risen over this period from 51.9 percent in 1968
  to 84.6 percent in the first four months of 1972 (computing this share
  as described above, which assumes that all Department of Agriculture
  units are for moderate-income households). Hence, the share of low-
  income units in total new subsidized production has dropped sharply to
  around 15 percent in the first four months of 1972.
- The Section 221 (d)(3) below market interest rate program and the
  Section 202 housing for the elderly program have been almost completely phased out. They have been replaced by the Section 236
  program.
- Although total production of new directly subsidized units rose rapidly
  from 1968 to 1970, it leveled off in 1971 and seems to be declining in
  1972. If the total for 1972 is 3.5 times that for the first four months
  (as was true for all housing starts in 1971), then it will be about
  317,000 units, or 27 percent below that for 1971. The same basic

pattern of rise, leveling, and decline appears to be occurring concerning
rehabilitated units.

- To meet the full decade target of six million subsidized units by 1978,
HUD originally planned on accelerating production from 300,000 units
in fiscal year 1969 to 800,000 units in fiscal year 1976. The production
schedule has since been altered to reflect the actual creation of directly
subsidized units in the last four years. If the six million goal is to be
reached, production in the next six years would have to be 161 percent
above the fiscal year 1972 total of 470,000 units. Thus, there would
have to be a very dramatic change in present trends if the target were
to be met by 1978.

- Housing subsidized by the Department of Agriculture has accounted for
slightly under one-sixth of all subsidized units created in this period—
including 15.7 percent of all newly built units, and 30.8 percent of all
rehabilitated units. Moreover, the USDA share of newly built subsidized
units has risen significantly in 1972, although it is too early to know
whether this will be true for the year as a whole.

Notes

1. Joint Economic Committee staff study, *The Economics of Federal Subsidy
   Programs* (Washington, D.C., January 11, 1972), p. 31.
2. *Ibid.;* and Henry J. Aaron, "Income Taxes and Housing, *American Economic Review* (December 1970), pp. 789–806.
3. Aaron, "Income Taxes and Housing."
4. Letter to Real Estate Research Corporation from Office of the Deputy
   Under Secretary, Department of Housing and Urban Development, August
   16, 1972.
5. Total public assistance payments in 1970 were $14.5 billion. Medical assis-
   tance was $5.5 billion, leaving $9.0 billion for all other uses. We roughly
   allocated one-third to housing. See *U.S. Statistical Abstract–1972,* p. 299.
6. Subcommittee of the Committee on Appropriations, U.S. House of Representatives, *HUD-Space-Science Appropriations for 1972: Hearings, Part
   3, Department of Housing and Urban Development* (Washington, D.C., 1971),
   p. 133.
7. See table 2–4 and Subcommittee on HUD-Space-Science-Veterans, Committee on Appropriations, U.S. House of Representatives, *HUD-Space-
   Science-Veterans Appropriations for 1973: Hearings, Part 3, Budget Amendments, Department of Housing and Urban Development* (Washington, D.C.,
   1972), p. 440.
8. Data taken from table 2–2.
9. Table 2–4.
10. "Conventional" in this sentence means "conventionally constructed" rather

than mobile homes, and does not refer to "conventionally financed" as opposed to FHA insured.

11. Data supplied by the Department of Housing and Urban Development.

12. Low-income households are defined in this study as those with incomes at or below the levels that qualify them for public housing occupancy. A rough approximation for a four-person household would be an annual income of $4,000 or less as of 1972. Moderate-income households are defined as those above the low-income level, but with annual incomes too low to enable rental or purchase of decent quality housing without direct subsidies. For a four-person family, this annual income range would be approximately $4,000 to $8,000 as of 1972.

3

The Magnitude of the Nation's Present and Future Housing Needs, and the Costs of Meeting Them

Size of the Nation's Present Financial Housing Needs

1. *Financial housing needs* have been estimated by The Urban Institute in calculations concerning a possible housing allowance. The number of households exhibiting such needs, and the total dollar amount involved, vary depending upon how certain terms are defined. Consequently:
   - Estimates of the number of households who would have needed financial assistance in 1969 in order to occupy decent quality housing without paying more than a "normal" fraction of their incomes range from 12.8 million to 18.3 million.[1]
   - Estimates of the total spending required in 1969 to meet such needs vary from $5.1 billion to $7.8 billion in 1969 dollars.
   - For purposes of this study, we used the midpoint in the above cost range, updated to 1972. *We therefore estimate that* fully *meeting the nation's financial housing needs as of 1972 would cost about $7.1 billion per year in some form of housing allowance or direct income maintenance.*[2]
2. Certain aspects of what the above statement really means should be clarified as follows:
   - "Fully meeting the nation's financial housing needs" immediately would not necessarily place every American household in "a decent home" in the near future. Rather, it would provide added housing purchasing power for every household that cannot now afford decent quality housing without spending an "abnormally high" fraction of its income on housing. The translation of such added housing purchasing power into actual occupancy of decent housing would take many years as private markets responded to this big injection of additional housing demand.
   - The cost estimate of $7.1 billion covers one year only, but any program designed to meet the nation's financial housing needs would really involve commitment to a program of assistance that would probably last indefinitely. This conclusion is discussed later in this section.
   - Programs meeting the nation's financial housing needs less fully than the one costed above would require smaller annual expenditures. Almost any desired annual cost level could be generated by changing the design

of the programs concerned. For example, The Brookings Institution has proposed one such program costing $3.0 billion as of 1976.[3]

Size of the Nation's Present Physical Housing Needs

1.   *Physical housing needs* were the basis for the official national housing goals in the 1968 Housing and Urban Development Act. Hence, those goals provide a measure of how much additional housing the nation would have to produce to meet its physical housing needs fully as of 1978. The following conclusions may be drawn:
     ● *Physical housing needs would be fully met by the production of 26 million additional decent quality dwelling units from 1968 to 1978, or an annual average output of 2.6 million units over ten years.*
     ● Actual production averaged 2.121 million units per year during the first three years of this specified ten-year period (1969 through 1971, including mobile homes). Hence, total housing production must average 2.805 million units per year in the remaining seven years to reach the target.
     ● Physical housing needs could also be met by a program that extended more than ten years from initiation to final target date. Such a program would require lower annual average outputs. However, it would also take longer to arrive at the time when all physical housing needs would be met.

2.   The official national housing goal includes production of six million directly subsidized units during the same decade. During the first three years, 354,000 directly subsidized units were produced per year, on the average. Hence, an average of 705,000 directly subsidized units per year must be produced in the remaining seven years to reach this target.

3.   Certain aspects of what the above statements really mean should be clarified as follows:
     ● "Fully meeting the nation's physical housing needs" means providing enough decent quality housing units, and locating them appropriately, so that there is one such unit for every American household (plus additional ones for normal vacancy). However, it does not necessarily imply provision of any financial aid to those households who could not afford to occupy such units without paying "abnormally high" fractions of their incomes to do so. The occupants of the six million additional directly subsidized units would receive such financial aid; so would occupants of directly subsidized housing units constructed before 1969. But millions of other low- and moderate-income households would not be receiving such aid.
     ● Although the programs set forth by the 1968 Housing and Urban Development Act would (if achieved) fully meet the nation's physical hous-

ing needs *as of 1978,* additional such needs would be generated in every year after that. This is discussed further below.

Estimating the Magnitude of Present Housing Needs Involves Calculations over Long Periods into the Future

1. The housing that every household needs consists of a continuous stream of services providing shelter and associated amenities, not just a building. Each household needs to consume such a stream not only today, but again every day into the future as long as the household lasts. Hence, "meeting housing needs" for any household is really a process that extends over time. Actions that provide housing services for the household, or help it overcome its own deficiencies in doing so, only for one day—or one year— do not "meet its housing needs" in any true sense.

2. This requirement to meet continuing housing needs as part of a long-range process is just as true for the entire nation as for each individual household. However, it has different meanings concerning the two basically different concepts of "housing needs" used in this study.

    *   *Financial housing needs* arise out of the "gap" between a "normal" fraction of a household's income appropriate for housing and the prevailing cost of occupying a decent quality dwelling unit (as defined by society). The main cause of this gap is poverty, as pointed out earlier. Slightly less than half of all the households in the United States officially defined as "poor" cannot earn their way out of poverty. Their members are either too old, or disabled, or small children, or mothers who must care for such children. Hence, any program that sets out to meet some or all of the financial housing needs of such households is assuming a financial burden that will last as long as such households exist. In modern industrialized societies, there is certain to be a significant number of such households at all times. That is why initiation of a program committed to meeting any part of financial housing needs amounts to assumption of a permanent financial burden of significant proportions. Therefore, the cost of such a program cannot be accurately stated in terms of a one-year amount. It must be seen as a continuing stream of costs extending indefinitely into the future. The complexities of estimating the total costs involved are discussed below.
    *   *Physical housing needs* arise because some of the occupied housing units in the nation's inventory fail to meet socially acceptable minimum quality standards. At first glance, it appears that this deficiency could be cured once and for all by creating enough new decent quality housing units to replace all those inadequate ones (or rehabilitating the latter) and to meet future population growth needs. That is precisely

the objective of the national housing goals, which seek to attain this "ideal outcome" as of 1978. Yet even if that heroic task were successfully completed, programs to meet physical housing needs would still have two major links to the long-range future beyond 1978. They are:

a. Under present programs, the federal government will directly finance the interest subsidy on most of the new units needed by 1978. Payment of these funds will continue up to forty years beyond the date of construction. If the loan is successfully repaid, the interest subsidy will continue to the end of the loan term. In case of foreclosure, the mortgage would be assumed by the government. Hence, the federal government is committed to a continuing interest in the viability of the units long past 1978.

b. In the years after 1978, the nation's population will continue to expand, and its older housing units will continue to deteriorate. Hence, additional physical housing needs will keep on arising past that date. It is not very likely that the federal government—having just finished a massive effort to meet physical housing needs through 1978— will then stop all action aimed at meeting additional such needs that arise after 1978. Thus, existing programs devoting significant resources each year to meeting physical housing needs probably represent a long-range commitment to continue doing so well beyond 1978.

On the other hand, Congress has been willing to virtually ignore these needs for long periods in the past. This could happen again—even before 1978. Also, if physical housing needs were fully met by 1978, the accumulated supply of deteriorated units would have been removed. Therefore, only those units reaching the end of their effective economic lives in any subsequent year would have to be replaced to keep the supply of housing current. The private unsubsidized market could be expected to maintain the balance to a large degree.

3. Thus any meaningful attempt by the federal government to meet either financial or physical housing needs represents a commitment to spend significant amounts of federal money each year for an indefinite period into the future.

Rough Projections of Total Costs of Meeting the Nation's Physical and Financial Housing Needs

1. It is extremely difficult to compare the total long-range costs of fully meeting the nation's physical housing needs with those of fully meeting its financial housing needs for the following reasons:

- "Fully meeting housing needs" means entirely different things when applied to physical needs and when applied to financial needs. Hence, any cost figures derived for these two actions do not really apply to comparable activities or to the production of comparable benefits.
- Estimating total lifetime costs in both cases requires forecasting the relative rates of speed at which personal incomes and housing costs will rise over long periods in the future—as far away as fifty years. No one can do this with much reliability.
- Future cost and revenue figures should be discounted to present values to avoid misleading comparisons of present and future magnitudes. Yet there is no established method of choosing what discount rate to use. In this study, we have used discount rates of 5.0 percent (approximately the federal government's borrowing cost) and 10.0 percent (the rate officially required by the Office of Management and Budget).

2. In spite of these difficulties, HUD and others have publicized partial estimates of the long-range costs of achieving the national housing goal of creating six million subsidized units from 1968 through 1978. To put these estimates in reasonable perspective, we have prepared our own extremely rough estimates of the "total costs" of fully meeting both basic types of housing needs.

- Our cost estimates for "fully meeting physical housing needs" were based upon HUD's calculations of the *most likely* future subsidy costs of achieving its share of the six million unit target. These estimates assume that many subsidy recipients would experience decreasing per-unit subsidies because their incomes rose faster than housing costs. Hence, these estimates are much lower than the *maximum possible* future subsidy costs if all Section 235 and 236 units remained at the highest possible per-unit subsidy throughout their lifetimes.

  These "lifetime" costs cover a period of fifty years forward from 1968, but we have tabulated only those costs incurred from 1972 onward through the year 2011. (Only minor costs are incurred after that date.)

- Our cost estimates for "fully meeting financial housing needs" were based upon the assumption that a nationwide housing allowance program would cost $7.103 billion as of 1972, and would be continued *annually* into the future through the year 2011. The annual current cost was assumed to (1) rise three percent per year (which it would if *both* incomes and housing costs rose at that rate), or (2) decline one percent per year (which it would if incomes rose faster than housing costs).

- Based upon the above assumptions, we estimate that the total costs of "fully meeting" these two types of needs through 2011 are as shown in table 3–1.

- The following conclusions can be derived from table 3–1:

  a. The total cost of fully meeting either type of housing needs seems

Table 3-1

Discounted Present Value of Total Subsidy Costs
from 1972 through 2011 (Billions)

Programs	5% Discount Rate	10% Discount Rate
HUD Subsidies for 5.0 Million Units	$ 55.8	$ 32.7
Total Subsidies for 6.0 Million Units* (Including Department of Agriculture)	$ 67.0	$ 39.2
Housing Allowance 1% Annual Decline 3% Annual Rise	$112.5 $200.1	$ 70.0 $103.6

*1.2 times HUD subsidies alone.
Source: Real Estate Research Corporation.

quite expensive. However, the amount is small compared to the
total cost of other federal budget items treated in the same way. For
example, if the total national defense costs of roughly $80 billion in
1972 declined one percent per year through 2011, the discounted
present value of total defense costs from 1972 through 2011 would
be $1,267 billion at a five percent discount rate (more than the
entire 1971 gross national product) or $787 billion at a ten percent
discount rate.

b. Fully meeting financial housing needs is significantly more expensive than fully meeting physical housing needs, regardless of which
discount rate is used, or which version of the housing allowance is
used. This fact should be kept in mind by those who advocate replac-
ing some or all construction-oriented subsidies with a housing allowance.

c. One reason why the housing allowance program costs more than the
construction-oriented subsidies is that the housing allowance would
continue paying households throughout the forty-year period; whereas the construction-oriented subsidies would continue building new
units only through 1978. Nevertheless, construction-oriented subsidies
also continue providing benefits for forty years. Some of their mortgage payments continue that long, and many of the housing units built
in 1978 and earlier would still be providing shelter forty years later.

• *It should be emphasized that these conclusions are tentative.* The cost
estimates shown in table 3-1 cannot be considered very reliable because
of the inherent uncertainties involved in making forty-year projections.

• Other programs involving less than fully meeting either physical or
financial housing needs would naturally cost less than the figures shown

in table 3–1. Thus, any one of many different combinations of total cost and "degree of total needs met" could be adopted if desired.

Notes

1. John D. Heinberg, *The Transfer Cost of a Housing Allowance: Conceptual Issues and Benefit Patterns* (Washington, D.C., May 1971), p. 55.
2. Housing allowance cost estimates do not include possible inflationary impacts on housing prices. It is presumed that an adequate supply of housing units would be provided, but the addition to the money demand for housing would probably raise costs if there were no direct construction subsidies.
3. Charles L. Schultze, Edward R. Fried, Alice M. Rivlin, and Nancy H. Teeters, *Setting National Priorities: The 1972 Budget* (Washington, D.C., 1971), p. 294.

4

The Effectiveness of Specific Forms of Housing Subsidies

General Approach to Evaluating the Effectiveness of Specific Housing Subsidies

1. Evaluating the effectiveness of specific housing subsidies is extremely difficult because (1) housing subsidies serve so many different objectives, (2) most current federal housing subsidy programs are mixtures of several different "pure forms" of subsidy, and (3) the actual impacts of each subsidy program are influenced more by *the way in which it is administered* than by the *inherent characteristics of the particular subsidies* it contains.

2. To cope with these difficulties, our general approach to evaluating specific housing subsidies consisted of the following steps:
    *   Identification of twelve "pure forms" of housing subsidies that could theoretically be used to reduce housing costs to the occupants. These are set forth in chart 4-1.
    *   Identification of eighteen specific criteria of desirability representing traits that it would be advantageous for any housing subsidy to exhibit. Most are generally desirable for all government expenditure programs. The eighteen criteria are also shown in chart 4-1.
    *   Construction of a theoretical housing situation based upon actual costs and characteristics of both rental and owner occupancy *without any public assistance whatever.*
    *   Evaluation of each "pure form" of subsidy in terms of its performance in the theoretical situation described above. For each form of subsidy, we measured the occupancy cost reduction achieved per dollar of subsidy cost. We also measured the effectiveness of each form of subsidy in relation to the quantifiable criteria of desirability.
    *   Application of subjective judgment to determine the extent to which each "pure form" was effective in meeting the remaining criteria.
    *   Identification of twenty-two existing federal housing subsidies and determination of the "pure forms" of housing subsidies contained in each, and the way in which they are combined. These are set forth later in this section.
    *   Identification of three alternative forms of federal housing subsidies that might be used instead of existing forms. These are: a below market interest rate subsidy program with a fixed interest rate (for which we used the 221 (d)(3) program as a model), a housing allowance paid to

27

Chart 4–1

Components of Evaluation of Specific Forms of Housing Subsidies

Theoretically Possible "Pure Forms" of Housing Subsidies	*Specific Criteria of Desirability Used in Evaluating "Pure Forms" of Housing Subsidies*
• Reduction of interest rate (as in the Section 235 and 236 programs).	• Administrative simplicity.
	• Ease of monitoring.
• Increase in loan coverage (as in the 221(d)(2) program).	• Low lifetime subsidy cost per housing unit.
• Payment of both principal and interest on a loan (as in public housing).	• Controlled or limited total cost.
	• Low annual federal budgetary cost per unit.
• Payment of direct capital grant to initial owner (not now in any program).	• Equity of impact among households with similar incomes.
• Payment of housing allowance to occupant (not now in any program).	• Equity of subsidy provided to households in similar quality units.
• Payment of housing allowance to building owner (as in the rent supplement, public housing leasing, and public housing operating cost aid programs).	• Focus of benefits on low-income households.
	• Full cost accountability.
	• Rapid production of benefits in relation to the timing of costs.
• Allocation for housing in general income maintenance (not now in any program).	• Adequate local government compensation for added costs.
• Allocation for housing in public assistance (as in welfare programs).	• Encouragement of operating cost efficiency.
• Deduction of mortgage interest and property taxes from personal income tax (as under present federal income tax laws).	• High ratio of federal costs to occupant benefits.
	• Low risk of federal repossession.
• Acceleration of depreciation for income tax saving (as in the Section 236 program).	• Ease of federal disengagement from the subsidy program.
	• Encouragement of maintenance and upkeep.
• Reduction of local property taxes (as in public housing).	• Possible future decline of subsidy cost per unit.
• Reduction of land costs (as in urban renewal).	• Reduced real cost to taxpayers if inflation continues.

Source: Real Estate Research Corporation.

the occupant, and a higher level income maintenance program with a negative income tax feature (like that proposed by the Heineman Commission).

• Evaluation of fifteen current federal housing subsidies and these three alternative subsidies to determine their effectiveness in meeting the

specific objectives of housing subsidies determined earlier, and the criteria of desirability described above.

- Identification and analysis of specific criticisms of federal housing subsidy programs as set forth in current literature on this subject, and as
discovered in our field research. Emphasis was placed on criticisms of
the Section 235 and Section 236 programs. This analysis is in Chapter 5.

- Development of conclusions about the overall effectiveness of current
federal housing subsidies and the three alternatives, based upon all of
the considerations described above, plus those set forth in other
chapters.

3.   This approach allowed us to analyze the characteristics of each "pure form"
of housing subsidy separately from its embodiment in existing programs.
Therefore, it was useful in deciding whether criticisms directed against each
existing subsidy program are really aimed at the *basic nature* of the subsidy
involved, or the *specific details* of the way it has been put into practice.

Results of the Evaluation of "Pure Forms"
of Housing Subsidies

1.   The results of our evaluation of the "pure forms" of housing subsidies
against the criteria of desirability are set forth in tabular form in chart 4–2.
It is a matrix, with criteria of desirability forming the rows, and specific
"pure forms" of housing subsidy forming the columns.

2.   Some of the main conclusions derived from chart 4–2 will be presented
later. However, the following are best set forth here:

- Every form of subsidy has both advantages and disadvantages—not one
is strongly effective without serious drawbacks. Hence, no "perfect" or
wholly noncontroversial housing subsidy programs can be devised. All
involve accepting certain disadvantages in order to gain certain advantages.

- Equity of impact by housing quality is not a sensible criterion for
evaluating any housing subsidies, since none achieves it. A frequently
quoted "deficiency" of new construction-oriented subsidies is that taxpayers who are not receiving them will resent knowing that some of
their neighbors living in exactly the same quality of dwelling as theirs
are getting public aid. This is an inescapable result of tying housing subsidies to household income levels, while requiring all households to live
in standard quality dwelling units. Precisely the same resentment could
arise against recipients of a housing allowance in older neighborhoods.
The only difference is that neighbors are somewhat less likely to know
who receives housing allowances.

- Low annual budgetary impact and low lifetime subsidy cost per unit

Chart 4-2

Effectiveness of 12 "Pure Forms" of Housing Subsidy in Meeting 18 Criteria of Desirability

Criteria	*Subsidy Forms*				
	Interest Rate Reduction	*Increase in Loan Coverage*	*Payment of Principal and Interest*	*Capital Grant*	*Housing Allowance to Household*
1. Administrative Simplicity	■	●	■	●	★
2. Easy Monitoring	■	●	■	●	★
3. Low Lifetime Subsidy Cost Per Unit	★	●	★	●	★
4. Controlled or Limited Total Cost	●	●	●	●	★
5. Low Annual Budgetary Cost Per Unit Aided	■	●	■	★	●
6. Equity of Impact by Income Level	★	●	★	★	●
7. Equity of Impact by Housing Quality	★	★	★	★	★
8. Focus of Benefits on Low-Income Households	★	■	■	●	●
9. Full Cost Accountability	●	NA	●	●	■
10. Rapid Production of Benefits in Relation to Costs	●	■	■	★	■
11. Adequate Local Government Compensation	●	●	●	●	●
12. Encouragement of Operating Cost Efficiency	●	●	●	●	★
13. High Benefit/Cost Ratio Related to Housing	■	●	●	★	★
14. Low Risk of Federal Repossession	■	★	●	●	●
15. Ease of Federal Disengagement	■	■	■	●	★
16. Encouragement of Maintenance and Upkeep	■	NA	■	●	●
17. Possible Decline of Per-Unit Subsidy Cost as Time Passes	★	★	★	★	■
18. Reduction of Real Subsidy Cost Per Unit if Inflation Continued	●	●	●	★	★

Code:　● Very effective　　■ Moderately effective　　★ Very ineffective

Source: Real Estate Research Corporation.

Housing Allowance to Rentor	Housing Allocation in Income Maintenance	Housing Allocation in Welfare	Personal Income Tax Deduction	Accelerated Depreciation	Reduced Property Taxes	Reduced Land Costs
★	●	●	●	●	●	★
★	★	★	●	●	●	★
★	★	★	★	●	★	★
★	★	★	★	●	●	●
●	■	■	●	●	●	★
■	●	●	★	★	★	★
■	★	★	★	★	★	★
●	●	●	★	■	●	★
●	★	★	★	★	★	★
■	■	■	■	■	●	■
●	●	●	●	●	★	■
★	★	★	●	●	●	●
★	●	●	★	■	■	●
●	●	●	●	■	■	●
■	★	★	★	●	●	●
●	●	★	●	★	■	★
■	★	★	★	●	★	■
★	★	★	★	●	★	■

NA   Not applicable

are almost mutually exclusive traits for any subsidies with positive costs. Hence, criticizing any specific form of subsidy for its failure to meet one of these criteria amounts to praising it for success in meeting the other, and vice versa.

- Most "pure forms" are built around either tying the subsidy to the debt incurred in initally constructing a housing unit, or tying the subsidy to the "gap" between some fraction of the occupant's income and the cost of occupying the unit. For example:

  a. *Debt-tied subsidy forms* include interest rate reduction, extension of loan term, increase in loan coverage, payment of principal and interest, and capital grants.

  b. *Income "gap" -tied subsidy forms* include housing allowances, rent supplements, and allocations within income maintenance and welfare programs.

  c. Personal income tax deductibility and accelerated depreciation subsidies are related to *both* debt and incomes.

- Debt-tied subsidies are limited in total amount and annual payment size, have definite expiration periods (when the debt is paid off or the property refinanced), and (except for capital grants) decline in real cost per year to the taxpayers if inflation continues, since they involve fixed annual payments.

- Income "gap" -tied subsidies have several major disadvantages in relation to debt-tied subsidies. Specifically:

  a. They have no built-in cost limits per household, and could therefore rise to indefinitely large sizes in the future if housing costs rose faster than consumer incomes (unless Congress changed the rule to prevent this). Hence, *they would probably not have declining real costs to the taxpayers if inflation continued.*

  b. They have no predetermined end point for each household, unless its income rises above program limits. If this does not happen, any household admitted to the subsidy program can receive aid as long as it exists. Moreover, other households in similar poverty are sure to become eligible in the future. Therefore, *once any such subsidy program is established, it is very likely to become permanent* (as welfare programs have).

  c. *They create little incentive for the household or the housing supplier to economize on housing costs.* The government automatically pays the difference between a certain fraction of the occupant's income and its housing costs. However, this drawback could be reduced if payments were keyed to an average housing cost for some set of households as a whole, or were otherwise limited in maximum amount.

  d. *They would probably require continuous administrative monitoring of both household income and housing unit quality.* Debt-oriented subsidies usually require certification of housing quality only at the time of the initial transaction, and may not require monitoring of household income at all.

e. They add directly to the money demand for housing, but do not directly increase the supply—hence, *they could have inflationary impacts upon housing prices.* These subsidies rely on the responsiveness of the private housing market to increase supply after they increase demand. Experience with medical demand subsidies shows that such reliance may not work.

f. *Much of the money spent on them would increase the general purchasing power of the recipients, rather than improve their housing quality.* Hence, such subsidies are really more antipoverty than antipoor-housing in nature.

- On the other hand, income "gap"-tied subsidies have certain advantages in relation to debt-tied subsidies, as follows:

a. *They focus benefits more strongly upon low-income households.* Their size is related to household income, but that of debt-tied subsidies is related to the cost of the housing unit concerned.

b. *At the program scale required to provide aid for every eligible household, these programs would involve lower subsidy costs per household aided.* Hence, they would also provide lower annual federal budgetary costs, though the costs would be permanent rather than limited to the length of loan terms. (Up to now, no federal housing subsidies have ever been funded at anywhere near this large a scale.) Physical housing needs would not be met through income "gap"-tied subsidies alone.

c. *They involve no risks of federal involvement in repossessing housing units and thereby sustaining foreclosure and resale losses.*

- Many current federal housing subsidies are mixtures of both debt-tied and income "gap"-tied subsidy forms, with one or the other dominant. Hence, each has some features of both types, but is dominated by the features of one. However, several current subsidies are entirely one type or the other. In each case, the subsidy program involved exhibits the basic characteristics of the dominant type.

- The classification of all major subsidies is as shown in chart 4-3.

Nature and Coverage of Current Federal Housing Subsidies

1. The major current federal housing subsidy programs—both direct and indirect—are briefly described in the Appendix. We have set forth only the most important current subsidy programs, and have described them in terms of

Chart 4-3

Classification of Debt-Tied and Income "Gap"-Tied Subsidies

Combination of Debt-Tied and Income "Gap"-Tied with:		One Type Only	
Debt-Tied Dominant	Income "Gap"- Tied Dominant	Entirely Debt-Tied	Entirely Income "Gap"-Tied
Section 235 (all versions)	Rent Supplements (all versions)	Conventional Public Housing	Public Housing Operating Cost
Section 236 (all versions)	Public Housing Leasing	Turnkey Public Housing	Housing Allow- ance to Occupants
	Accelerated Depreciation	Section 221 (d)(3)	Higher Income Maintenance
	Income Tax Deductibility	Rehabilitation Loans	

Source: Real Estate Research Corporation.

the "pure forms" of subsidy they contain, plus other major characteristics. A great many details and variations are omitted.

2. Chart 4-4 arrays most of these current federal housing subsidy programs by the housing types and income levels they cover. Housing types are broken down into homeownership and rental occupancy categories, with new con- struction, existing units, and rehabilitated units included in each. The result- ing six housing types are further broken down into three income levels each. Within each of the eighteen boxes thus formed are shown the current fed- eral housing subsidies that reduce occupancy costs for at least some house- holds in the indicated income group for the indicated housing type.

3. The percentage of all households in each income group shown in chart 4-4 who actually receive each indicated housing subsidy varies from nearly 100 (for middle- and upper-income households owning new homes) to nearly zero (for low-income households owning new homes). Hence, the presence of a certain subsidy in any box does not necessarily mean that most or even many of the households in that category actually benefit from that subsidy.

4. The following conclusions can be drawn from chart 4-4:
    *   Some type of federal housing subsidy is at least theoretically available to nearly all income groups in relation to all types of housing except for (1) middle- and upper-income renters, (2) moderate-income renters of existing units, and (3) low-income owners of rehabilitated and exist- ing units (the subsidies theoretically available to low-income owners of units have been provided to so few households they can be ignored).
    *   Low-income renters theoretically have more options concerning dif- ferent types of federal housing subsidies than any other group.
    *   The easiest subsidy to obtain administratively, and the one that covers

Chart 4-4

Existing Housing Subsidy Coverage, by Housing Type and Income Level

Household Income for 4-Person Family***	Home Ownership			Rental Occupancy		
	New Units	Existing Units	Rehabilitated Units	New Units	Existing Units	Rehabilitated Units
Middle- and Upper-Income	Income tax Deductibility	Income tax Deductibility	Income tax Deductibility	Accelerated Depreciation† (200%)	Accelerated Depreciation† (125%)	—
$8,000						
Moderate-Income**	Section 235	Section 235	Section 235 Sections 115*, 312*	Section 236	—	Section 236 5-year Write-off
$4,400						
	Public Housing-Turnkey III		Sections 115*, 312*	Public Housing -Conventional -Turnkey -Leasing -Oper. cost	Public Housing -Leasing -Oper. cost	Public Housing -Leasing -Oper. cost
Low-Income	Mutual or Self-Help			Rent Supplement* -Market -With Sec. 236		Rent Supplement* -Market -With Sec. 236

* Qualifications other than income required.

** Sections 502 and 515 provide coverage similar to Sections 235 and 236 respectively for areas with populations of under 10,000.

*** Incomes higher in a few high-cost areas.

† Subsidy goes to *owners* of rental units but presumably results in *somewhat* lower rents than would occur without it.

Source: Real Estate Research Corporation.

the highest percentage of those theoretically eligible for it, is the income tax deductibility subsidy. It provides benefits mainly to middle- and upper-income homeowners, rather than to poor households. This subsidy is also by far the largest in total dollars, as pointed out earlier. Hence, *the present federal housing subsidy structure as a whole does not focus its benefits mainly upon low-income households, but provides even more complete coverage of middle- and upper-income households* (especially since a high proportion of the latter are homeowner occupants).

Results of the Evaluation of Major Current Existing Federal Housing Subsidies

1.   The results of our evaluation of major current existing federal housing subsidies, plus three likely alternatives, against *both* the objectives of housing subsidies and the criteria of desirability are set forth in tabular form in charts 4-5 and 4-6. These charts are matrices similar to the one concerning "pure forms" of subsidies described earlier, and use the same symbols. In addition, we have summarized these charts in table 4-1. It shows the percentage of both objectives and criteria concerning which each existing form of federal housing subsidy was considered very effective, moderately effective, or very ineffective (cases of nonapplicability were omitted in computing these percentages).

2.   Two aspects of these effectiveness ratings should be emphasized:
   *   We attempted to rate each subsidy program in terms of its inherent potential if administered in ways that would maximize that potential, rather than its current impact as now administered.
   *   The percentages shown in table 4-1 have been computed without weighting individual objectives or criteria—which is the same as weighting them all equally. Undoubtedly, they are not all of equal importance. Hence, these percentages should be considered only roughly suggestive of the relative effectiveness of these subsidy programs; they are not precise measures.
   *   To weight the objectives and criteria would add a second level of subjectivity (the first being the ranking in charts 4-5 and 4-6). A great deal of caution must be used, however, in evaluating the unweighted results shown in table 4-1. Because of the need to arrive at some relative ranking of subsidy programs, we have included this table. The subsequent commentary takes into account the limitations of such an unweighted tabulation.

3.   The following conclusions can be drawn from charts 4-5 and 4-6 and the unweighted summary in table 4-1:

Table 4-1
Unweighted Results of Evaluating Specific Housing Subsidies Against 14 Objectives and 18 Criteria of Desirability

| | Percentage of Effectiveness Ratings for Each Subsidy By Degrees of Effectiveness in Relation to: | | | | | | | | |
| | Nine Primary Objectives | | | All 14 Subsidy Objectives | | | All 18 Criteria of Desirability | | |
Specific Subsidy Programs	●	■	★	●	■	★	●	■	★
Section 235									
New construction	63	12	25	54	23	23	39	33	28
Rehabilitated	38	37	25	31	31	38	39	22	39
Existing	25	25	50	23	23	54	39	22	39
Section 236									
New construction	56	11	33	50	21	29	39	39	22
Rehabilitated	25	37	38	23	31	46	33	34	33
Public Housing									
Conventional	44	11	45	36	7	57	39	17	44
Leasing	44	11	45	36	14	50	33	39	28
Turnkey	45	22	33	36	28	36	44	17	39
Operating cost subsidy	22	22	56	14	22	64	17	0	83
Rent Supplement									
New construction	56	22	22	43	28	29	17	50	33
Existing	44	11	45	29	14	57	22	45	33
With Section 236	45	22	33	43	28	29	22	45	33
Rehabilitation—Sections 115 and 312	50	12	38	46	8	46	50	17	33
Income tax deductibility	22	11	67	22	14	64	39	6	55
Accelerated depreciation	11	22	67	14	22	64	50	22	28
Section 221(d)(3) BMIR	50	12	38	38	31	31	50	11	39
Housing allowance to occupant	38	50	12	31	38	31	33	17	50
General income maintenance plus negative income tax	25	50	25	23	39	38	44	6	50

Code: ● Very effective ■ Moderately effective ★ Very ineffective

Source: Real Estate Research Corporation.

Chart 4-5

Effectiveness of 18 Existing and Proposed Actual Forms of Housing Subsidy in Meeting 14 Objectives*

	1 Section 235 – New Construction	2 Section 235 – Rehabilitation	3 Section 235 – Existing	4 Section 236 – New Construction	5 Section 236 – Rehabilitation	6 Public Housing – Conventional	7 Public Housing – Leasing (Existing)
Primary Objectives							
1. Assisting Low-Income Households by Improving Units	■	■	■	■	■	●	●
2. Assisting Low-Income Households by Raising Incomes	★	★	★	★	★	★	●
3. Assisting Moderate-Income Households by Improving Units	●	●	●	●	●	★	★
4. Assisting Moderate-Income Households by Raising Incomes	★	★	★	★	★	★	★
5. Assisting Special Groups in Need	NA	NA	NA	●	NA	●	●
6. Encouraging Home Ownership	●	●	●	★	★	★	★
7. Stimulating the Economy	●	■	★	●	■	■	★
8. Increasing Total Supply of Decent Housing Units	●	■	★	●	■	●	■
9. Improving Deteriorated Neighborhoods	●	●	■	●	●	●	●
Secondary Objectives							
10. Stabilizing Housing Industry Output	■	★	★	■	★	★	★
11. Encouraging Innovations	■	★	★	★	★	★	★
12. Creating Economic Opportunity in Poor Areas	★	●	■	■	●	●	★
13. Encouraging Participation of Private Resources	●	■	●	●	■	★	■
14. Achieving Spatial Dispersion	●	★	★	●	★	★	●

Code: ● Very effective   ■ Moderately effective
       ★ Very ineffective   NA Not applicable

*The first two primary objectives have been subdivided to separate physical and financial housing needs. The objective of providing college housing is omitted. Consequently, there are 14 objectives instead of 13.

Source: Real Estate Research Corporation.

8	9	10	11	12	13	14	15	16	17	18
Public Housing — Turnkey	Public Housing — Operating Cost	Rent Supplement — New Construction	Rent Supplement — Rehabilitation	Rent Supplement — With Section 236	Sections 115 and 312 Rehabilitation Aid	Income Tax Deductibility for Owner-Occupancy	Accelerated Depreciation on Housing	Section 221(d)(3) Below Market Interest Rate	Housing Allowance Paid to Household	General Income Maintenance with Negligible Income Tax
●	■	●	●	●	●	★	★	■	■	■
★	●	●	●	■	★	★	★	★	●	●
★	★	★	★	★	●	★	★	●	■	★
★	★	★	★	★	★	★	■	★	●	■
●	●	●	●	●	NA	★	★	NA	NA	NA
■	★	●	★	●	●	●	★	★	■	■
■	★	■	★	■	★	■	★	●	■	■
●	★	■	■	★	■	●	●	●	★	★
●	■	●	●	●	●	★	■	●	●	●
★	★	★	★	★	★	■	★	■	★	★
★	★	★	★	●	★	★	★	★	★	★
■	★	■	★	■	●	★	■	■	●	●
●	★	●	■	●	●	●	●	●	■	■
■	■	■	★	■	★	★	★	■	★	★

Chart 4–6

Effectiveness of 18 Existing and Proposed Actual Forms of Housing Subsidy in Meeting 18 Criteria of Desirability

	1	2	3	4	5	6	7
Criteria of Desirability	Section 235 – New Construction	Section 235 – Rehabilitation	Section 235 – Existing	Section 236 – New Construction	Section 236 – Rehabilitation	Public Housing – Conventional	Public Housing – Leasing (Existing)
C-1 Administrative Simplicity	■	★	★	■	★	★	■
C-2 Easy Monitoring	■	★	★	■	★	★	■
C-3 Low Lifetime Subsidy Cost Per Unit	★	★	★	★	★	★	★
C-4 Controlled or Limited Total Cost	●	●	●	●	●	●	■
C-5 Low Annual Budgetary Cost Per Unit Aided	■	■	■	■	■	■	■
C-6 Equity of Impact by Income Level	★	★	★	★	★	★	★
C-7 Equity of Impact by Housing Quality	★	★	★	★	★	★	★
C-8 Focus of Benefits on Low-Income Households	■	●	●	■	●	●	●
C-9 Full Cost Accountability	★	★	★	★	★	★	●
C-10 Rapid Production of Benefits in Relation to Costs	●	●	●	●	●	●	●
C-11 Adequate Local Government Compensation	●	●	●	●	●	★	●
C-12 Encouragement of Operating Cost Efficiency	■	■	■	●	●	●	■
C-13 High Benefit/Cost Ratio Related to Housing	■	■	■	●	■	●	●
C-14 Low Risk of Federal Repossession	★	★	★	■	■	■	●
C-15 Ease of Federal Disengagement	●	■	■	■	■	■	■
C-16 Encouragement of Maintenance and Upkeep	●	●	●	■	■	●	■
C-17 Possible Decline of Subsidy Cost Per Unit	●	●	●	●	■	★	★
C-18 Reduced Real Cost if Inflation Continues	●	●	●	●	●	●	★

Code: ● Very effective   ■ Moderately effective
        ★ Very ineffective   NA Not Applicable

Source: Real Estate Research Corporation.

8	9	10	11	12	13	14	15	16	17	18
Public Housing — Turnkey	Public Housing — Operating Cost	Rent Supplement — New Construction	Rent Supplement — Rehabilitation	Rent Supplement — With Section 236	Sections 115 and 312 Rehabilitation Aid	Income Tax Deductibility for Owner-Occupancy	Accelerated Depreciation on Housing	Section 221(d)(3) Below Market Interest Rate	Housing Allowance Paid to Household	General Income Maintenance with Negligible Income Tax
■	★	★	★	■	■	●	●	■	★	★
★	★	★	★	★	●	●	●	●	★	★
★	★	★	★	★	●	★	●	★	★	★
●	★	★	★	★	●	★	●	●	★	★
■	★	■	■	■	★	●	●	●	●	●
★	★	★	★	★	★	★	★	★	●	●
★	★	★	★	★	★	★	★	★	★	★
●	●	●	●	●	■	★	■	★	●	●
★	★	■	●	★	●	★	★	★	■	●
●	●	●	●	●	★	■	■	●	■	■
★	★	●	●	●	●	●	●	●	●	●
●	★	■	■	■	●	●	●	●	★	●
●	★	■	■	■	■	★	★	●	★	★
●	●	■	■	■	●	●	■	★	●	●
■	★	■	■	●	●	★	★	■	★	★
●	★	■	■	■	●	●	★	●	●	●
★	★	■	■	■	★	★	●	★	■	★
●	★	■	■	■	★	★	■	●	★	★

- Three objectives of housing subsidies are rather poorly served by all existing subsidy programs. They are (1) assisting moderate-income households with financial housing needs by raising their incomes, (2) stabilizing the output of the housing industry, and (3) encouraging innovations. Only the first of these would be well served by any of the alternative subsidy programs: a housing allowance paid to the occupants.

- All of the other eleven objectives of housing subsidies are well served by several existing subsidies, but no one subsidy—existing or proposed—serves all of them well. Nor does any one subsidy serve all eight remaining primary objectives very effectively. This indicates that an "optimal" set of housing subsidies should include several different types, rather than just one.

- Subsidies that serve moderate-income households directly also provide some benefits to low-income households. This occurs through the "chains of moves" started by households who move into units newly furnished by those subsidies. In contrast, subsidies that serve low-income households directly do not provide benefits to moderate-income households.

- Except for rehabilitation loans and grants and accelerated depreciation, none of the current federal housing subsidies has low lifetime costs per housing unit covered. This failing would also be true of a housing allowance or higher income maintenance, though they would be paid to households rather than units. This situation reflects the high cost of enabling relatively low-income households to occupy housing conforming to the existing high level quality standards in the United States.

- Administration and monitoring pose significant difficulties concerning almost all current or proposed federal housing subsidies—except for accelerated depreciation and tax deductibility subsidies.

- No housing subsidy program inherently achieves equity of impact by income levels. Whether any would do so depends upon the magnitude of funding Congress provides for it. We have rated a housing allowance and higher income maintenance as very effective concerning this criterion because both are usually proposed as available to all eligible households. But there is no inherent reason why a housing allowance in particular might not be limited to households living in certain areas, or certain types of housing. In that case, it would be very ineffective at meeting this criterion. Conversely, all other housing subsidies would be effective at meeting it if sufficiently funded by Congress to aid everyone eligible.

- Few current housing subsidies provide full accountability. Most contain some tax reduction benefits that do not appear in the federal budget.

- All current housing subsidies (except rehabilitation grants) produce benefits rapidly in relation to their incurrence of costs. We believe this illustrates congressional awareness that current dollars are more valuable than future dollars, and therefore implicitly supports the use of discounting in calculating future program costs.

● Public housing programs (except leasing) impose a serious penalty upon local governments by compelling them to provide tax abatement.

● Most current housing subsidies have been deliberately designed so that per-unit subsidy costs might decline in the future under certain conditions. (Even the tax deductibility subsidy might decline if the standard deduction is increased in size.) However, public housing programs are not likely to experience such a decline.

● The aggregate results of unweighted effectiveness ratings are shown in chart 4-7.

Chart 4-7
Summary of Results of Unweighted Effectiveness Ratings*

Subsidy Effectiveness in Relation to Subsidy Objectives		Subsidy Effectiveness in Relation to Criteria of Desirability	
Most Effective	Least Effective	Most Effective	Least Effective
Section 235 New	Accelerated Depreciation	Accelerated Depreciation	Income Tax Deductibility
Section 236 New			
	Public Housing Operating Cost	Section 235 New	Public Housing Operating Cost
Rent Supplement			
		Section 236 New	
Rehabilitation Aids	Income Tax Deductibility		
Section 221 (d)(3)		Rehabilitation Aids	
		Public Housing Leasing	
Housing Allowance			
Turnkey Public Housing			

*The rankings of "very effective" and "moderately effective" are added together to determine the most effective subsidies.
Source: Table 4.1.

4.   Overall, the subsidies that this analysis shows as having the greatest net effectiveness are Section 235 new construction, Section 236 new construction, and rehabilitation aids. However, it should be emphasized again that this conclusion is based upon weighting all objectives and all criteria equally, and they are undoubtedly not all of equal importance.

Conclusions Concerning the Effectiveness of Specific Current Housing Subsidy Programs

1.   After performing the theoretical evaluation of existing and proposed housing subsidies described above, we also analyzed their practical results and

the problems and criticisms each has encountered. (The major criticisms are discussed in chapter 5. Our conclusions about the overall effectiveness of the major existing individual subsidy programs are set forth below. Specific recommendations for future changes in existing programs are presented in chapter 8.

2. On balance, we believe that both the Section 235 and Section 236 programs are effective instruments for meeting the key objectives of housing subsidies. They represent rather ingenious blends of "pure forms" of subsidies designed to incorporate the advantages of several types. We believe that their basic designs are sound, although some modifications can improve them. The major inadequacies so far encountered in the execution of these programs have stemmed mainly from either poor administration by HUD or the inherently higher risks of investing capital in housing for relatively low-income households in relatively deteriorated areas. Such higher risks are inescapable in any meaningful attempts to achieve the basic objectives of housing subsidies.

   - A preponderant majority of the more than one-half million housing units made available under these programs have been of good quality and have been well received by both their occupants and the surrounding communities.

   - Both these programs combine the debt-tied subsidy advantages of limited total amount, definite terminal date, and declining real cost if inflation occurs with the income "gap" -tied subsidy advantage of declining amount when occupant incomes rise faster than housing costs.

   - Because these are moderate-income rather than low-income programs, both are well suited for achieving at least some degree of economic integration, since persons with a relatively wide range of incomes can participate (especially in the Section 236 program when rent supplements are added). This is a crucial advantage for achieving some economic integration in new-growth neighborhoods.

   - Initial experience indicates that a significant percentage of households who start receiving these subsidies earn their way out of them through higher incomes. In the latest recertification of incomes for Section 235 housing, 8.0 percent of all subsidy receivers stopped getting any subsidy, 65.8 percent received a reduced subsidy, 13.4 percent had no change, and 20.8 percent received a larger subsidy. There is no actual experience yet on Section 236 rise-out rates.

   - The fact that these programs provide profitable incentives for builders and investors to undertake them is an advantage, not a disadvantage. It stimulates participation of private capital, and has helped generate vastly greater production of subsidized units than ever before.

3. Our net assessments of the other major current housing subsidy instruments are as follows:

   - *Public housing conventional and turnkey programs are fundamentally sound instruments for providing decent physical dwelling units for households with low incomes but no major social problems.* However, their effectiveness in meeting *shelter-oriented* objectives has been distorted because our society has used them as instruments for trying to cope with certain *non-shelter problems* that are best dealt with through other types of programs that have so far not been adopted in adequate form or volume. The most significant of these non-shelter problems are poverty, destructive behavior by members of some households, and the negative environmental results of requiring large numbers of low income households to live concentrated together by deliberately excluding them from the middle- and upper-income areas.

a. These public housing programs deliver housing services rather well in many smaller communities across the nation.

b. Their fundamental deficiency in large cities is that they tend to concentrate large numbers of very poor households together. We believe such concentrations are both socially and economically non-viable, and create destructive environments.

- The proportion of all public housing occupants receiving some form of public assistance (other than Social Security) rose from 21 percent in 1955 to 54 percent in 1971. This indicates the increasing concentration of economically dependent households in such housing.

- These concentrations cannot be avoided as long as (1) large-scale public housing projects already exist, (2) society refuses to develop other effective means of providing housing for very poor multi-problem households, and (3) courts prevent housing authorities from screening out or ejecting such households.

- Furthermore, such concentrations make public housing projects unsound economically, since the occupants cannot afford to pay enough rent even to cover operating costs. That is why Congress created the public housing operating cost subsidy, which is discussed separately below.

c. The only way to achieve successful deconcentration of the very poor in the long run is to create alternative scattered housing units in which such households can live. Public housing conventional and turnkey programs should continue to be used as one of the instruments for this purpose, though not the only or even the primary one.

- This means all additional conventional and turnkey public housing units should be created in small-scale projects at scattered locations.

- We believe all central-city public housing authorities should be allowed to operate on a metropolitan areawide scale without restriction to the boundaries of the central city.

  Relative emphasis concerning public housing should shift from conventional and turnkey programs to public housing leasing of existing units, with maximum feasible scatteration throughout each entire metropolitan area.

d. Present public housing programs unfairly penalize local governments by paying inadequate amounts in lieu of local property taxes. The federal government should provide a more adequate per-unit subsidy in lieu of taxes paid to local governments. It should be a per-unit amount close to what such units would pay if market rents were charged and assessments were made under normal local practices. This new subsidy should be financed entirely by the federal government as part of its annual contribution, over and above debt service payments.

e. Another fundamental deficiency in present public housing programs is the excessive number of relatively small, probably inefficient local housing authorities engaged in creating and managing public housing units. It would be more efficient to have a single local housing authority covering each metropolitan area, and perhaps one state-wide authority for all communities outside of metropolitan areas. Legislation encouraging consolidation of smaller authorities by providing strong operating cost benefits for doing so might produce this result.

f. The basic advantages of these public housing programs in comparison with a housing allowance paid directly to the households concerned is that public housing expands the housing supply and provides administrative oversight concerning housing, which many low-income households need because of their own bargaining inexperience or incapacities. Hence, we believe these programs will continue to have a significant role in meeting housing subsidy objectives.

g. Whether these public housing programs should be expanded in large cities depends upon society's policy choices concerning non-housing objectives, rather than the effectiveness of these programs as housing instruments per se. How are we going to provide for the basic needs of multi-problem low-income households—and cope with the problems they generate for others? These are the crucial questions, although few political leaders or government officials are willing to confront them.

● *The public housing operating cost subsidy is, in our opinion, a fundamentally unsound instrument of public policy.* This subsidy pays the difference between the actual operating costs of public housing projects and 25 percent of the occupants' incomes. It radically alters the normal relationship between management and occupants in a way that reduces management's ability to help sustain viable environments in public housing projects. Many tenants pay no rent at all; and in some cases, the management actually pays the tenants each month (when very poor tenants pay their own utility bills). This situation removes nearly all economic incentive for careful property maintenance. It also disrupts tenant morale by causing variable rental treatment of tenants in identical units. Finally, it removes most incentives for either management or tenants to economize on resources used for operating costs.

a. We believe this subsidy should be abolished as soon as it can be replaced by more adequate income maintenance paid to public housing occupants by some agency other than HUD or the local housing authority.

b. An even better substitute for this subsidy would be creation of a wider range of income groups living in public housing projects, so that some households there could pay rents that would fully cover operating costs. Therefore, we recommend that no households be ejected from public housing projects because of incomes above stated limits if they are willing to remain and pay certain minimum rents. Such rents should be equal to either about 25 percent of their incomes (varying with household size) or an amount equal to their prorated share of all operating costs plus some add-on percentage contribution to debt service, whichever is lower.

● *The public housing leasing program and the rent supplement program represent potentially very effective instruments for achieving several key objectives of housing subsidies.* They have the major advantage of allowing individual low-income households to live "blended in" with other households without special designation as subsidy recipients. They also allow scatteration of assisted households in many areas, thereby avoiding some of the difficulties caused by excessive concentration of the poor. However, to realize their potential most effectively, these programs need major changes in present rules.

a. Public housing leasing should be freed from the requirement that the community where it is located have a local housing authority. Moreover, local public housing authorities in every central city should be authorized to use this program anywhere within the metropolitan area where they are located, as noted above.

b. The following changes should be made in the rent supplement program:

 ● It should be more generally applicable to existing standard-quality units, not just new or rehabilitated units.

 ● Households who receive the subsidy in a given unit, and then earn higher incomes and become ineligible, should be eligible again if their incomes fall back into the permissible range. At present, they have to move out.

 ● The workable program requirement, and all other requirements for specific community approval, should be abolished.

● *The large size of the income tax deductibility subsidy, relative to all others combined, creates what we believe is an unbalanced overall housing subsidy structure.* Moreover, this subsidy is extremely ineffective in meeting those subsidy objectives related to assisting low- and moderate-income households. However, it provides substantial benefits to large numbers of middle- and upper-income homeowners. Since they constitute a majority of Americans, there is a very high probability that this subsidy will be retained in the future.

a. The objectives this subsidy serves effectively are encouraging home-ownership, encouraging participation of private resources in housing, increasing the supply of decent dwelling units, and stimulating the construction industry.

b. It is probably undesirable—or even impossible—to reduce this subsidy greatly because of its political popularity. Therefore, moving towards a more properly balanced overall subsidy structure would require expanding those housing subsidies benefiting low- and moderate-income households. The proportion of the income tax deductibility subsidy that benefited households with incomes under $7,000 was only 10.2 percent in 1966, as shown in table 4–2.

c. We believe it would be especially unfortunate if Congress decided to reduce the total amount of resources used for housing subsidies by cutting back on those highly visible subsidy programs that benefit the relatively poor, while leaving untouched this vastly larger—but less visible—subsidy that benefits the relatively affluent.

Table 4–2
Tax Savings from Deductibility of Mortgage Interest and Property Taxes By Income Groups, 1966

Income Group	Tax Savings	Percentage of Total Tax Savings	Cumulative Percentage of Total Tax Savings
	(Millions)		(Top Downwards)
Over $100,000	$ 79	2.7%	2.7%
$50,000–$100,000	$ 139	4.8%	7.5%
$25,000–$ 50,000	$ 305	10.5%	18.0%
$15,000–$ 25,000	$ 595	20.5%	38.5%
$10,000–$ 15,000	$ 892	30.7%	69.2%
$ 7,000–$ 10,000	$ 597	20.6%	89.8%
$ 5,000–$ 7,000	$ 188	6.5%	96.3%
$ 3,000–$ 5,000	$ 91	3.1%	99.4%
Under $3,000	$ 19	0.6%	100.0%
Total	$2,905	100.0%	

Source: Henry Aaron, The Brookings Institution.

5

The Validity of Major Criticisms of Current Direct Housing Subsidy Programs

We have identified and analyzed about eighty-six specific criticisms of federal housing subsidy programs, including both general criticisms and those directed at particular subsidies. The first section of this chapter deals briefly with the most important criticisms of the Section 235 and 236 programs. Then the general criticisms of subsidy programs are discussed in seven sections, each of which is devoted to a major critical point.

Specific Criticisms of the Section 235 and 236 Programs

1. The specific criticisms of these programs fall into three categories, each of which has different implications for the desirability of continuing or modifying these programs. They are as follows:

Basic Category of Criticism	*Nature of Implication*
Attacks on the *basic nature* of the subsidy involved.	They question the desirability of continuing this program without
Attacks on the *way the subsidy program is being administered*.	major modifications in basic nature. They indicate the desirability of changing administrative rules,
Attacks on *deficiencies of resources* used in the subsidy program.	procedures, or criteria. They indicate the need for supplemental resources or services.

2. Both the largest number of criticisms, and those that appear to be most accurate and most warranting changes in present practices, concern the *agree* ways in which these programs have been administered. These criticisms can be answered by changes in administrative practices without altering the basic nature of the subsidy programs concerned.

3. Many of the most telling criticisms of program administration were made by HUD audit analysts themselves. HUD has already responded with many changes in administrative rules, regulations, and practices. Further changes were continuing when this study was prepared.

4. We have listed in charts 5-1 and 5-2 the main administrative criticisms of both programs that we believe are (or were) at least partly valid. Responsive changes in administration are easily derived from them; so we have not

49

Chart 5-1

Valid or Partly Valid Criticisms of the Section 235 Housing Subsidy Program
Concerning its Administration and Resource Deficiencies

Criticisms of the Program's Administration

- Regarding the use of Section 235 for existing homes:
  - —FHA appraisals were inadequate and failed to catch many needs for major repairs.
  - —Inflated values were placed on many units because of poor appraisals and failure to check on past sales of the same units.
  - —Many poor households were led to believe that an FHA appraisal was a guarantee of quality, and FHA did little to discourage this belief through effective informing of buyers.
  - —Poor appraisals resulted in excessive subsidy costs to the government and large losses of income and even defaults by buyers.

- HUD has inadequate income certification and recertification procedures.

- HUD could save money by eliminating handling fees for recertifying, or at least reducing them.

- More formal minimum income requirements should be established so that every buyer has enough income to cope with heating, maintenance, utility, and other operating costs as well as debt service.

- Subsidies for existing homes have been used to underwrite the rapid entry of relatively low-income families (mostly black) into previously all-white neighborhoods through home purchases—thereby essentially financing the "flight" of white households from central cities.
  (Note: We believe this criticism applies mainly to Section 221(d)(2) loans and other nonsubsidized programs, rather than Section 235 loans.)

- Too high a proportion of new units are being built in areas outside the lowest income neighborhoods where they are needed most; hence, they are not serving the people who need them most.
  (Note: We were unable to obtain accurate information concerning the location of Section 235 units nationwide, but we believe this criticism is partly valid on the basis of admittedly sketchy evidence.)

- Homeowners under this program receive a double subsidy because they can deduct that portion of the mortgage interest paid by the government from their federally taxable income.
  (Note: This can be viewed as an advantage of the program, since it further reduces occupancy costs.)

- Long-term financing through direct loans from the federal government, or federally-guaranteed bonds issued by the Federal National Mortgage Association (FNMA), should be substituted for present "normal" FNMA financing of Section 235 loans. FNMA's nonguaranteed bonds require higher interest rates than would government-guaranteed bonds, or direct government loans. The difference in interest rates may be as large as two percent—which adds tremendously to the lifetime subsidy costs.

Criticisms of Resource Deficiencies

- Households receiving this subsidy should be provided with much more extensive counseling on how to care for homes and meet other responsibilities of homeownership.

Source: Real Estate Research Corporation.

described them here. Valid or partly valid criticisms concerning resource deficiencies are also shown on the charts.

5. Inadequate administration has been the main cause of recent housing scandals concerning inner-city areas. Yet these scandals and defaults related to them have been widely construed as indicating that current direct housing subsidy programs are "failing." We believe this interpretation is false for the following reasons:

- Most of the scandals involved excessively high appraisals and purchase costs or high repossession rates of existing older housing in deteriorated central-city neighborhoods. The particular housing insurance programs involved are mainly nonsubsidized programs being used under Section 223 or Section 237 terms (which allow normal loans to persons unable to qualify for normal credit, or in high risk areas). Only a small percentage of all these defaults involved Section 235 loans. We believe most of those concerned older existing units—not newly-built ones.

- If FHA had fully carried out all the steps in its loan approval regulations, most of the excessive valuations involved in these cases would not have been approved for mortgage insurance. This hardly indicates any failure in program design.

- The probability that administrative inadequacies would arise in the handling of housing programs concerned with inner-city areas has been greatly increased by three factors beyond the control of FHA officials themselves. These factors can be summarized as follows:

  a. Congress has immensely increased the number of subsidized housing units that must be processed by HUD, and greatly raised the percentage of those units requiring far more complete inspection than was typical of nonsubsidized units. HUD executives also put great pressure upon FHA offices to speed up processing of loan insurance in inner-city areas. Yet Congress and the Office of Management and Budget have at the same time reduced HUD's total staff.

  - In 1966, HUD's total permanent staff was about 14,000. It rose to 15,200 by the end of fiscal 1972. This is a net rise of about 8.5 percent in six years. From 1966 to 1971, the annual number of subsidized housing units produced in the United States rose 521 percent, and the annual number of housing units produced under FHA nonsubsidized insurance programs increased 80 percent. The number of local public housing authorities to be dealt with rose 62 percent.

  - Inspecting and processing are much easier for units newly built in subdivision tracts than for older existing units individually financed in inner-city areas. Yet a significant percentage of FHA's workload shifted from the former to the latter in this period.

Chart 5-2
Valid or Partly Valid Criticisms of the Section 236 Housing Subsidy Program Concerning its Administration and Resource Deficiencies

Criticisms of the Program's Administration

- HUD's review and certification of project costs has been inadequate, and has caused the government to include excessive costs in subsidized mortgages.

- In many projects, operating expenses have been initially calculated at far too low levels. This results in sponsor demands for rent increases, or needs for additional sponsor cash inputs, right after initial occupancy. It has even caused some defaults.

- Nonprofit sponsors are not required to have any significant equity; hence, they cannot cope with high operating costs and often get into default.

- HUD does not renegotiate commitments once made, even though market conditions can change and make units nonfeasible long before they are built or even before construction has started.

- HUD has inadequate income certification and recertification procedures.

- Quality of management is one of the most crucial determinants of project success, but HUD does not investigate this trait very thoroughly beforehand or place high priority upon it in deciding who should receive allocations. Nor does HUD follow up to see that management is being carried out properly.

- Section 236 projects have too often been clustered together because HUD has not paid attention to their likely cumulative effects upon local market conditions. This has resulted in excessive vacancies in some cases.

- HUD does not put enough emphasis upon the past "track record" of sponsors in determining who will receive allocations. More such emphasis would encourage stronger interest in project management over the long term by sponsors.

- Income limits should not be tied to public housing income limits because local public housing authorities sometimes deliberately manipulate public housing income limits to reduce the number of eligible families. Section 236 income limits should be tied to local median family income—such as 80 percent of that median.

- Long-term financing through direct loans from the federal government, or federally-guaranteed bonds issued by the Federal National Mortgage Association (FNMA), should be substituted for present "normal" FNMA financing of Section 236 loans. FNMA's nonguaranteed bonds require higher interest rates than would government-guaranteed bonds, or direct government loans. The difference in interest rates may be as large as two percent—which adds tremendously to the lifetime subsidy costs.

- There should be minimum income limits so that occupants will not be spending very high fractions of their incomes for housing. These limits should apply to rent supplement units as well as those without rent supplement (though different limits should be used in these two cases). The limits established by HUD in February 1972 restrict tenants to those who will not pay more than 35 percent of their adjusted incomes for basic rent. This policy should be reexamined as incomes are recertified.

Criticisms of Resource Deficiencies

- Section 236 units are not being built with enough amenities to keep them competitive with nonsubsidized housing in the future, or to attract and retain households who do not need to receive the subsidies involved. They need air conditioning, carpets, swimming pools, and other such amenities.

- Not enough social services are provided in some projects, such as security forces, tenant counseling, etc.

Chart 5–2 (continued)

Criticisms of Resource Deficiencies (continued)

- Community public relations programs should be mandatory, especially where rent supplement units are included, so as to minimize friction with surrounding property owners.

- Quality of some sites has been low, as marginal land was used. HUD allows such sites to be used, and local governments tend to restrict subsidized housing to marginal sites to keep them out of "better" neighborhoods.

  (Note: We were unable to obtain accurate information about where Section 236 projects are located nationwide. However, our field checks indicate this criticism may be true in some places.)

- Insistence upon a mixture of units in each project with and without rent supplements—with latter in majority—inhibits use of this program in two types of areas:
  —In very low-income neighborhoods, non-rent-supplement households cannot be persuaded to live with those needing rent supplements. Closer to 100 percent allowance of rent supplements would make housing available to those who need help most—especially in rehabilitated units.
  —In middle-income areas, need to obtain local legislative approval for rent supplement units prevents use of the program in many communities that have deliberately avoided adopting workable programs to block subsidized housing. Where 100 percent non-rent-supplement projects are built, the program can be used in such communities anyway.

- Not enough Section 236 projects are being built in low-income areas within central cities where the needs are greatest.

  (Note: We were able to check where Section 236 units are being built in only a few areas, but they indicate that most are being built within central cities but not in the lowest income neighborhoods.)

Source: Real Estate Research Corporation.

- It is apparent that the basic personnel policies imposed upon HUD by Congress and the Office of Management and Budget have been totally inconsistent with the expanded responsibilities given this department.

b. The Department of Housing and Urban Development has undergone several major reorganizations in the past few years. The most recent involved decentralization of personnel, and a large-scale rotation in both geographic areas and functions. As a result, many of the persons responsible for processing specific types of housing insurance applications in each FHA office were unfamiliar with either that particular type of housing, or the housing industry and developers in the area they were serving. This reorganization greatly reduced the efficiency and effectiveness of FHA offices at the same time that their workload was expanding and becoming more complex. It generated a high propensity to make errors, cause undue delays, and overlook possible problems likely to arise from dealing with unscrupulous real estate operators, and with home buyers unfamiliar with homeownership.

    c. Although most FHA personnel were trained in processing loans to highly credit-worthy borrowers living in good quality neighborhoods, FHA's workload has shifted to much greater emphasis upon marginally credit-worthy borrowers living in marginal or low quality neighborhoods. Hence, many FHA personnel are not familiar with the types of problems now facing them. Yet until very recently, little serious effort was made to train FHA personnel concerning the new types of problems they were sure to encounter as a result of this shift.

6. Most criticisms of the basic nature of the Section 235 and Section 236 programs have proven upon examination to be either false or capable of being responded to effectively without fundamental changes in program design. However, some changes in these programs do appear warranted. We have set forth these criticisms in charts 5–4 and 5–5, along with our assessment of their validity and the changes they appear to justify. In addition, certain more general criticisms of housing subsidy programs relevant to Section 235 and Section 236 operations are dealt with in later sections of this chapter (for example, the charge that default rates are excessive).

**General Criticisms of Existing
Housing Subsidy Programs**

The general criticisms of federal housing subsidies identified in our research have been grouped for discussion into seven major critical points, most of which represent groupings of a number of specific criticisms. These points are shown below.

Chart 5–3
Major Criticisms of Current Housing Subsidy Programs

These criticisms contend that such programs, as now constituted and operated, exhibit:

- Excessive total budgetary costs.
- Too much emphasis upon new construction.
- Too many foreclosures and repossessions.
- Enrichment of builders and other intermediaries at taxpayer expense.
- Inequitable and incomplete coverage of low-income groups.
- Exploitation of the poor.
- Inflationary impact upon housing costs.

In this section, we present each of these seven critical points as a set of often-

Chart 3→

Most Significant Criticisms of the Basic Nature of the Section 235 Housing Subsidy Program

Criticism	Brief Evaluation of Criticism	Real Estate Research Corporation Comments
1. Rehabilitation is cheaper than new construction in providing shelter for large families; hence, new construction should not be used because it is inefficient.	Premise is true; but conclusion drawn is false.	Even though rehabilitation does provide more space per dollar invested, it is probably not possible to get production of rehabilitated units high enough to meet the needs Section 235 was made to serve. Also, only new units can achieve dispersal and certain other subsidy objectives.
2. Prices of some new Section 235 units are higher than those of comparable new conventionally financed units (before the subsidy is applied); hence, the program is inherently inefficient.	Premise may be true; but does not invalidate program.	Evidence is very limited, but we believe any program involving extensive government regulations is likely to be more costly than one free of such regulations. Also, new conventionally financed units at lower prices are not available in any large quantity; so their price is strictly theoretical.
3. Households with incomes that qualify for Section 235 cannot really afford homeownership; therefore, many Section 235 units will eventually be returned to the government through default.	Probably false; and would not invalidate program even if true.	There have been low default rates in the program up to now; so this seems false. Even if such rates get much higher, a majority of households using this program will still benefit from it, and the losses from repossession are not excessive when resale amounts are taken into account. This criticism indicates that a minimum income would be a good idea, however.
4. Builders do not have any long-range interest in the housing units because they sell out quickly; hence they do not invest enough in high quality construction in the first place.	May be true of a few builders, but not of most. Would not invalidate program even if true.	Builders who want to continue doing business with HUD must establish a good track record; hence, they do have a continuing interest in the quality of their current projects. However, a stronger warranty for builders in general might be desirable to help protect buyers.
5. Subsidizing new units exactly like nonsubsidized Section 203 units nearby causes unequal treatment of families in identical housing, and generates resentment among occupants not receiving subsidies but paying taxes to help those who do receive them.	True; but same problem is inherent in all housing subsidy programs.	This situation results from tying subsidies to household incomes, but requiring all households to occupy relatively high quality housing units. It is inherent in all housing subsidy programs, and cannot be avoided. Only its visibility is greater under the Section 235 program when joined with Section 203.

Chart 5-5

Most Significant Criticisms of the Basic Nature of the Section 236 Housing Subsidy Program

Criticism	Brief Evaluation of Criticism	Real Estate Research Corporation Comments
1. There is no real incentive for anyone to exercise good on-going management of Section 236 projects over the long run. Many sponsors are in the business of forming projects and selling out to investors. The investors are interested only in tax shelter, and the major shelter benefits end in about ten years. Hence, there is a strong chance that management quality will decline, and even that FHA will have to take back many projects after about 10 years.	Premise is partly true; but conclusion only partly valid. Some changes in program are warranted.	Investor incentive to avoid foreclosure after ten years is stronger than most people realize, because foreclosure is treated as sale at the mortgage amount for tax purposes. Since the mortgage amount is higher than the depreciated amount after ten years, this would cause a big capital gains liability for the investors. Also, sponsors interested in continuing to do business with FHA want to avoid a record of inadequate management or foreclosure. Nevertheless, we believe some improvement in management incentives is warranted. Initial sponsors might be required to retain a permanent interest of 20 to 25 percent rather than being allowed to sell out fully to investors.
2. The so-called "market rent" in Section 236 projects (the subsidized rent plus the subsidy) is actually higher than the *true* market rent for comparable nonsubsidized units nearby. This indicates program inefficiency. It also means that households with rising incomes will not remain in 236 units when their subsidies fall—as the program assumes— but will move out, because they can get better housing for the same price elsewhere. This will cause excessive concentration of relatively low-income households in 236 projects, making them less feasible and less integrated economically.	Premise is true; and conclusion is valid. But criticism does not invalidate program.	We believe this criticism is largely correct. Section 236 units cost more than comparable nonsubsidized units nearby because those nearby units are mainly older existing ones built when costs were lower, or they did not have to go through government red tape and regulations, or meet FHA quality standards. Nevertheless, Section 236 does expand the supply of moderate-income housing, and often provides the only newly built housing in some older low-income areas. The only way to correct this situation is to allow more amenities in such units to begin with—but this might raise rents even higher.
3. Rehabilitation is cheaper than new construction in providing shelter for large families; hence, new	Premise is true; but conclusion drawn is false.	Even though rehabilitation does provide more space per dollar invested, it is probably not possible to get produc-

Criticism	Assessment	Response
construction should not be used because it is inefficient.		...tion of rehabilitated units high enough to meet the needs Section 236 was made to serve. Also, only new units can achieve dispersal and certain other subsidy objectives.
4. Developers of Section 236 units are encouraged to build as expensively as possible rather than to be efficient because their fees are tied to the size of the mortgage amount, which depends upon costs.	Premise and conclusion both true; but this is probably an unavoidable trait.	We believe this criticism is valid, but the situation is almost inescapable. It might be possible to set flat fees per unit for building Section 236 units, but that would encourage construction of small units, whereas large families have the greatest unmet needs. Hence, there are some advantages in having fees tied to total cost.
5. Developers can gain more profit, or no less profit, from dealing with relatively higher income households in good quality neighborhoods than from dealing with relatively lower income households in much lower quality areas—although the latter need housing aids much more. Hence, present program encourages "creaming" by developers rather than focusing upon greatest needs.	Premise and conclusion both true. Some change in program warranted.	We believe this criticism is valid, and warrants some change in the program. Present rate of return on invested capital (including tax shelters) seems adequate to attract investors to less risky projects. But there should be a differentially higher rate for high-risk projects (those in deteriorated areas or with high fractions of poor tenants) than for lower-risk projects. Such a differential can be created by altering the Building and Sponsor Profit Allowance or other terms of the program.
6. Original operating costs are greatly underestimated to get project approval. Then when actual costs rise, developers get higher rents—making the units too expensive for many moderate-income households the program seeks to serve.	Premise and conclusion often both true. Needs both better administration and different funding emphasis.	This criticism is often correct. Two remedies are possible. One is more accurate cost estimation and certification review by FHA staff members. The other is using rent supplements with more Section 236 units to reach households who cannot afford higher rents.
7. Why should taxpayers provide housing subsidies for a small fraction of moderate-income households through an essentially horizontal redistribution of incomes? Why should only some households with incomes of around $4,400 to $8,000 per year be aided, but not most of them? Wouldn't it be better to concentrate aid on really poor households?	Premise that aid goes to limited percentage of eligible is true; but conclusion does not necessarily follow.	The basic answer to this natural question is that meeting the physical housing needs of all American households can best be accomplished by meeting the financial housing needs of just some households. Hence, one possible overall housing strategy is to subsidize units for some moderate-income households in order to meet national housing goals for physical housing needs. This question is dealt with more fully in another part of this section.

voiced questions. We then discuss the issue raised by each set of questions, and arrive at such conclusions as seem warranted from our entire study. It should be emphasized that the statements of the criticisms themselves represent the way they are usually heard—including all the errors they may contain. These statements do not necessarily represent our judgments on the issues concerned. It should also be emphasized that the conclusions in this section represent the judgments and opinions of Real Estate Research Corporation, based upon the considerations set forth in this study. These conclusions do not necessarily reflect the views of any of the organizations sponsoring this study, nor any of our other clients.

1. *Is it true that continued pursuit of the official national housing goals would result in very high "locked-in" budgetary costs by 1978—on the order of $5 to $8 billion per year? Could this outcome be avoided by using some other forms of subsidies?*

    - Exactly how large the annual budgetary costs of pursuing the official housing goals would be by 1978 is impossible to estimate reliably because of inherent uncertainties about future per-unit costs. However, if the national goals were actually achieved by 1978 by means of the programs now planned, we believe there would be a "locked-in" budgetary cost for housing subsidy payments in that year amounting to at least $5 billion, and perhaps as much as $7.8 billion.[1]

    - This does not mean that such a large annual cost would necessarily recur each year throughout the forty-year lifetimes of the longest mortgages involved, however. The annual cost could become smaller or somewhat larger than this as time passed, depending mainly upon how fast consumer incomes rose in relation to housing costs.

    - We do not believe there is any way to fully meet either the nation's financial housing needs or its physical housing needs without incurring an annual budgetary cost of this same order of magnitude as of 1978. The only way to avoid that level of cost is to refrain from fully meeting either type of housing needs. Shifting the form of subsidy to a housing allowance or to some type of income maintenance would alter program emphasis from meeting physical housing needs to meeting financial housing needs. This would result in more households being aided, and a lower subsidy cost per household. But it would not significantly reduce the total budgetary cost as of 1978 if financial housing needs were fully met. And it would commit the nation to a permanent program of household-oriented housing assistance similar to the welfare program. Furthermore, physical housing needs would not be met, and could be increased.

    - Whether it is worthwhile to incur such costs in order to meet either type of housing needs is, of course, a value judgment that must be decided politically and ethically. It cannot be decided scientifically.

- It should be pointed out that this annual budgetary cost as of 1978 might be smaller than the annual cost of the tax deductibility subsidy in that same year, although the latter would not appear in the federal budget. This subsidy equaled $5.4 billion in fiscal 1970, and $5.7 billion in 1971. Hence, it rose $300 million in one year, mainly because inflation moved many homeowning households into higher tax brackets. If this subsidy continued rising $300 million per year, it would equal $7.8 billion by 1978.[2]

2. *Is there an excessive emphasis upon new construction in existing subsidy programs? Why should we pay the high per-unit cost of putting low-income households into brand new units anyway? Wouldn't we be better off shifting to some form of subsidy that made more intensive use of the existing housing inventory for such households? Isn't that also fairer to taxpayers who have to foot the bill and cannot afford brand new housing themselves?*

- To put this issue in perspective, we must first point out that constructing at least some brand new units for low- and moderate-income households performs five important functions that cannot be achieved by helping them live in existing units. These functions are:

  a. *Expansion of the total housing supply so as to keep housing prices from rising.* Some such expansion becomes even more important if a housing allowance or other means of pumping purchasing power into low-income housing markets is adopted. Without a big expansion in total supply, much of that added purchasing power would be dissipated in rising prices. This would injure other households not receiving the housing allowance.

  b. *Achievement of some deconcentration of poverty in central cities, and some economic integration in new-growth areas.* Over two-thirds of our population growth will occur in new-growth suburbs during the next two decades. Low- and moderate-income households cannot live in older housing in these areas because all the housing is, by definition, brand new. Unless we want to exclude people in the lower half of the nation's income distribution from these new areas, we must use some type of subsidies applicable to brand new units.

  c. *Construction of certain types of units not existing in the inventory but needed by low-income households.* These include multi-bedroom units for large poor families, and conveniently located smaller units for elderly households.

  d. *Stimulation of increased activity in the construction industry.* This stated objective of housing subsidies is better attained through new construction than through rehabilitation or upgrading of older units, although the latter would have some expansionary effects.

  e. *Provision of dramatic, large-scale upgrading in older deteriorated areas.* Such upgrading can have two functions: (1) creation of a completely new environment in a highly decayed neighborhood through large-scale clearance and rebuilding, or (2) demonstration of social concern for the residents in a very low-income area by construction of a moderate-scale development that exhibits a "model" type of local environment.

- On the other hand, use of a housing allowance or other income mainte-nance-related subsidy to increase the housing purchasing power of a great many low-income residents of older neighborhoods all at once would perform some important functions that new construction-oriented subsidies cannot carry out. These are:

  a. *Provision of more adequate funds with which property owners (whether landlords or owner-occupants) could better maintain older properties.* This might help prevent older areas from deteriorating.

  b. *Spreading out housing assistance to a larger number of households than would receive new unit subsidies costing the same total amount.*

  c. *Allowing households themselves to engage in the search for, and negotiations about, individual housing units.* However, many such households could benefit from counseling services concerning how to do these things—just as those about to occupy new units need similar counseling.

- Several existing direct housing subsidy programs have many of the characteristics of a housing allowance, and could—if expanded—be used to perform the above functions. The public housing leasing program and the rent supplement program both have such capabilities. The former is especially suitable because experience has shown that it is relatively inexpensive per unit, easier and faster to administer, and easier to "blend" into existing neighborhoods than most new construction-oriented subsidies.

- In light of the above factors, we have arrived at the following conclusions concerning this issue:

  a. The housing program mix should contain both new construction-oriented subsidies and subsidies oriented toward more intensive use of the existing inventory.

  b. Although the present program mix does contain both types, emphasis has so far been much stronger on the new construction-oriented subsidies. Therefore, it would be desirable to move toward relatively greater emphasis on subsidies using existing units in the future. This could be done either by expanding the latter more than the former, or contracting the latter less than the former, depending on what is determined about the overall scale of housing subsidies.

  c. Existing subsidies capable of performing this function should be given relatively high priority for expansion—especially the public housing leasing program.

d. Experiments testing a housing allowance program that are presently underway should be continued, and given high priority attention. However, no full-scale version of such a program should be undertaken until more is known about its likely effects, if then. Past experience with welfare rent allowances shows that price rises are likely to absorb such allowances with little improvement in housing quality if no provisions are made to expand the supply directly available to the low-income households concerned.

e. Experiments should also be conducted to test a new program allowing low- and moderate-income households to rent single-family homes repossessed by FHA. The rent supplement and public housing leasing programs could be modified to allow this.

f. Adequate funds should be made available to provide counseling services for households using all these subsidies.

g. Requirements for specific local government approval prior to use of the public housing leasing program should be removed. Central-city public housing authorities should be empowered to lease units under this program within their own metropolitan areas but outside the boundaries of their own cities, so long as they do not concentrate many such units together.

h. Although any final decision should be postponed until the results of the above described experiments are obtained, we do not now believe that a nationwide housing allowance program providing assistance to all households eligible on the basis of low income alone would be desirable for three basic reasons:

- Most of the money spent in such a program would really be general income maintenance, not housing assistance. We believe the proper vehicle for such general assistance is an expanded income maintenance program.

- Adoption of such a program might cause Congress to reduce construction-oriented housing subsidies too far on the grounds that the nation's housing needs were "adequately taken care of" by the housing allowance. We believe there will continue to be a strong need for large-scale subsidies of newly-built units, for the reasons expressed earlier.

- The bigger the housing allowance program, the greater the upward pressure on the prices and rents of existing units. We believe it would be desirable to confine such a program to areas where the existing stock needs such a "shot in the arm," rather than creating such pressure throughout the nation.

3. *What are the default and repossession rates of current subsidy programs as compared to nonsubsidized programs? If subsidy programs have higher default rates, does that indicate they involve excessive risks? Will federal tax-*

payers be saddled with enormous future costs generated by large repossession and resale losses?

- Default-related statistics involve three different conditions as follows: [3]
  a. *In serious default* means a mortgage payment has not been made but the mortgage is still held by the mortgagee—there is no cost to the federal government.
  b. *Default termination* means a mortgage has been foreclosed or assigned to the Secretary of HUD.
  c. *Acquisition* means the title to a property has been legally transferred to HUD (usually FHA). HUD must then maintain the property, resell it, or demolish it—all at some cost to the taxpayer.

- These conditions are usually measured by the *number of units* in each condition, and *that number is stated as a percentage of all the units covered by insurance* under the program concerned at the beginning of the year. For example, in 1966, 38,744 units insured under Section 203 entered default termination. This number equaled 1.09 percent of all the units covered by insurance under that program at the beginning of 1966. [4]

- Default termination is a much more serious condition than default. Nearly all default termination units are eventually returned to HUD (although a small fraction are terminated by full payment by the owners). But among all defaulted units (including nonsubsidized units), only eight percent of multi-family units and about 25 percent of all single-family units come into HUD's possession. Most of the others are redeemed by full payment of delinquencies. [5]

- Default terminations and units in serious default for the major current direct subsidy programs, and for the largest FHA nonsubsidized insurance programs, are indicated in table 5-1. One section of the table covers single-family homes under homeownership programs; the other covers multi-family units, mainly under rental programs. The nonsubsidized programs have been included in table 5-1 as a basis for comparison with subsidized programs. Data are for selected (and representative) years from 1960 through 1968, and all years from then through 1971. The following conclusions can be derived from this table.
  a. In every year up to now, over 90 percent of all subsidized homeownership units insured have had no financial problems serious enough to cause even a missed mortgage payment.
  b. Section 235(i) units have the highest default and default termination rates, with the former totaling 4.55 percent and the latter 4.45 percent in 1971.
  c. These rates are significantly higher for subsidized programs than for the large-scale nonsubsidized Section 203 program. The latter's

Table 5-1

Default Terminations and Units in Serious Default—Selected Single- and Multi-family Programs, 1960-1971

Single-family Programs

Home Mortgage Default Terminations—Units, Number and Percentage of Insurance in Force at Beginning of Year

Year	Section 203 Number	%	Section 221(d)(2) Number	%	Section 235(i)* Number	%	Section 223(e) Number	%
1960	5,763	0.23	9,492	2.54	—	—	—	—
1962	25,330	0.87	6,710	2.18	—	—	—	—
1964	34,835	1.08	4,644	1.87	—	—	—	—
1966	38,744	1.09	4,591	2.11	—	—	—	—
1968	28,822	0.75	4,714	2.82	—	—	—	—
1969	21,255	0.53	2,465	3.23	41	—	25	0.36
1970	21,783	0.52	1,485	5.38	1,171	4.58	2,086	4.58
1971	18,705	0.44	400	3.17	5,766	4.45	3,326	4.67

Number of Units in Serious Default as Percentage of Insurance in Force

Year	Section 203 Number	%	Section 221(d)(2) Number	%	Section 235(i)* Number	%
1960	22,490	0.83	23,430	5.10	—	—
1962	40,592	1.32	15,919	4.27	—	—
1964	52,789	1.55	8,506	2.70	—	—
1966	52,520	1.41	5,282	2.13	—	—
1968	54,330	1.35	4,646	2.37	—	—
1969	60,368	1.45	2,257	1.94	140	0.53
1970	72,097	1.69	1,287	2.61	2,536	1.96
1971	82,562	1.90	835	3.89	12,300	4.55

Multi-family Programs

Home Mortgage Default Terminations—Units, Number and Percentage of Insurance in Force at Beginning of Year

Year	Section 207 Number	%	Section 221-MR Number	%	Section 221-BMIR Number	%	Section 236 Number	%
1960	1,754	2.68	930	26.06	—	—	—	—
1962	1,300	1.25	173	3.48	—	—	—	—
1964	3,916	2.66	190	3.80	484	3.76	—	—
1966	4,365	3.04	1,744	18.58	326	0.85	—	—
1968	2,812	1.94	402	2.40	122	0.16	—	—
1969	495	0.35	343	0.92	889	0.72	—	—
1970	846	0.60	499	0.80	3,139	1.98	—	—
1971	956	0.63	3,367	3.16	5,534	3.36	1,969	1.59

Number of Units in Serious Default as Percentage of Insurance in Force

Year	Section 207 Number	%	Section 221-BMIR Number	%	Section 236 Number	%
1960	1,356	1.64	—	—	—	—
1962	1,399	1.09	—	—	—	—
1964	3,003	1.97	326	1.21	—	—
1966	4,031	2.72	1,236	2.42	—	—
1968	1,003	0.71	4,171	3.36	—	—
1969	807	0.57	2,537	1.60	—	—
1970	1,650	1.08	8,049	4.88	841	0.68
1971	2,000	1.27	16,500	9.71	5,300	2.52

*Includes both newly constructed and existing units financed under Section 235.

Source: U.S. Department of Housing and Urban Development.

default termination rate averages below 1.00 percent, and its serious
default rate is below 1.90 percent—both less than half the averages
for subsidized programs.

d. For multi-family programs, annual default termination and serious
default rates for subsidized programs have generally been even lower
than those for subsidized homeownership programs. However, there
has been a recent increase in serious defaults among Section 221
below market interest rate units to 9.71 percent in 1971. In addition,
default terminations of Section 221 BMIR units totaled 3.36 percent
in 1971. This sudden rise from previous relatively low levels was
associated with earlier HUD pressure on FHA area and regional
offices to make large quantities of loans, plus oversupply and rising
expenses in real estate markets.

e. The highest default termination rates experienced in any multi-
family programs were in Section 221 market rate (*nonsubsidized*)
loans, which had rates of 26.1 percent in 1960 and 18.6 percent in
1966. In both cases, these proved to be one-year aberrations largely
caused by general economic conditions.

f. In most years, over 94 percent of all the units insured under any
multi-family subsidy program were experiencing no serious financial
difficulty.

• As of December 31, 1971, outstanding serious defaults for most homeownership programs were concentrated in just a few cities. The fifteen
jurisdictions with the highest defaults contained 60 percent of all those
in the nation—including 60 percent of Section 203 defaults, 79 percent of Section 221(d) (2) defaults, and 38 percent of Section 235
defaults.[6]

a. Of the 67,005 homeownership defaults in these areas, only 6.3 percent were Section 235 units. Of all homeownership defaults in the
nation at that date, Section 235 units comprised 10.2 percent. Moreover, a disproportionate share of those defaults concerned *existing*
homes insured under Section 235, rather than newly-built or rehabilitated ones.

b. Special tabulations concerning Detroit, which has the highest total
number of problem cases, indicate that only a small fraction of these
cases have arisen from Section 235 or Section 236 subsidies. Most
involve market rate loans with low down-payment requirements—so
low that when the owner must move, it is cheaper to abandon the
mortgage than to pay transfer costs and reclaim the tiny equity that
has built up.

• As of May 1, 1972, 4.8 percent of the 225,645 units insured under Section 236 were in default, and another 1.5 percent had been assigned to

or acquired by HUD. Thus, 93.7 percent were in no evident financial difficulty.[7]

Of the 109 Section 236 projects that entered default status from January through April 1972, 73 percent were nonprofit sponsored— although only 41 percent of all Section 236 projects had nonprofit sponsors. Thus, the default rate for nonprofit-sponsored units is about 9.4 percent—or almost four times as high as that for limited-dividend sponsors (2.5 percent).[8]

- When HUD must repossess a unit, it normally resells that unit at an over-all loss. From 1935 through June 30, 1972, HUD acquired 458,170 homeownership units, but sold all except 49,469. It acquired 108,297 multi-family units, selling all except 24,857. Thus, HUD had about 75,000 housing units in its possession as of June 30, 1972.[9]

  a. Only about 3.5 percent of these units originated in direct subsidy programs. Nearly all were 221 (d)(3) below market interest rate units.

  b. The average financial loss per unit through March 1972 was $5,172 for homeownership properties, and $2,037 for multi-family properties. However, the average loss per unit for Section 235 properties was $4,017.[10] The latter figure includes existing and new units financed under Section 235.

- In our opinion, these data do not indicate any tendency towards "massive" or even large-scale defaults or default terminations in current direct subsidy programs. Because such subsidy programs deal with households poorer than those covered by nonsubsidized programs, it is natural to expect the former to have somewhat higher default rates, as they do. Yet over 90 percent of all units created under these programs have been free from serious financial problems.

  a. From the beginning of all FHA programs through 1970, it cost the federal government about $1.4 billion to acquire and resell the 457,700 units it so handled because of its mortgage results in *all* programs. Since about 12.2 million units were insured under those programs, the default termination rate has been about 3.75 percent.[11]

  b. If there were a 5.0 percent default termination rate on all six million units to be subsidized under the programs aimed at reaching national housing goals, and the cost of handling and reselling was $3,000 per unit, the total cost would be $900 million. This is clearly a large amount, but it does not appear excessive in relation to past experience, considering the higher risk of dealing with lower income households. It amounts to $150 per unit over all six million units.

  c. This estimated future cost is much lower than some recently quoted in the press. They were based upon extrapolations from experience in Detroit, where abnormally high costs and default rates have occurred. Although default rates could rise higher than those projected above, we do not believe the situation in Detroit, which involved a compounding of many adverse factors, forms a reliable basis for such projections.

- Even if foreclosures occurred in subsidized programs at much higher rates than nonsubsidized programs—say as high as 25 or 50 percent of all subsidized units—this would not necessarily mean the subsidized programs were unsuccessful, or should be abandoned. Rather, it could be considered an addition to the net subsidy costs required to cope with the serious social and economic problems these programs were designed to attack.

  a. The annual subsidy cost of a Section 236 unit at maximum subsidy level is around $800 per year. Even if *50 percent of all* such units were repossessed once during their forty-year lifetimes and sold at an average loss per unit of $4,000, this would amount to an added subsidy cost of $2,000 per unit for *all* Section 236 units—or the equivalent of 2.5 extra years of annual subsidy payments. If such losses occurred in future years, their discounted present value would be even smaller.

  b. It is extremely unlikely that such high default and repossession rates will occur. But even if they did, this calculation indicates that they would not be nearly as undesirable as depicted in most press accounts.

- Another factor to consider regarding this issue is the present value of relatively low amenity housing built right after World War II for occupancy by veterans. Most of this housing has a market value today far larger than the cost of building it seventeen to twenty-five years ago. Its vulnerability to possible deterioration and obsolescence was very similar then to that of much subsidized housing being built now. However, long-range inflation in housing costs, and the general price structure, has more than offset this vulnerability. We believe there is a built-in political bias towards long-run inflation in the American economy. These forces are likely to operate in the future destiny of subsidized housing being built today.

4. *What proportion of the benefits of tax-supported housing subsidies go to builders, developers, investors, land owners, and other "intermediaries" rather than low- and moderate-income households themselves? Wouldn't it be less wasteful of taxpayers' money to pay needy households directly in cash and let them find their own housing? Isn't that less likely to enrich intermediaries at the expense of those in need?*

- This criticism contains both a partial truth about how present housing subsidies operate, and a major error about how they might operate under different arrangements. These are described below.

a. It is true that current programs provide benefits to "intermediaries," and that the cost of such provision is borne by taxpayers. It is also true that current programs pay federal funds directly to such "intermediaries" in nearly all cases, rather than directly to housing consumers.

b. However, it is a delusion to believe that any system of providing improved housing services to individual households can avoid dealing with "intermediaries"—that is, third parties other than the federal government and the households being aided. In reality, almost all housing services in the United States are supplied to housing occupants by "intermediaries" of some type. Third parties build units for homeowners and lend them the money to purchase those units. Third parties also build, finance, and manage units rented to nonowner occupants. Even public housing authorities are "intermediaries" in relation to the federal government and their tenants.

c. The reason why some households need housing assistance is that they lack the capability (usually the money) necessary to motivate these suppliers to provide them with adequate quality housing services. Hence, the essential purpose of all housing subsidies is to change the behavior of housing service suppliers—"intermediaries"—towards needy households. This purpose is just the same for a housing allowance paid directly to the occupant as it is for a bond subsidy paid to a local housing authority, or an interest subsidy paid to a mortgage lender. The occupant can improve his housing with such an allowance only if he uses at least part of it to pay higher rent to a landlord or a higher price for a single-family home than he could previously afford to pay. Naturally, no housing subsidy can accomplish this essential purpose without increasing the benefits that relevant "intermediaries" can derive from providing better services to the households being aided. Hence, stating that housing subsidies benefit "intermediaries" is not really a criticism. Rather, it is a description of precisely what the subsidies must do to accomplish their purposes.

• The relevant question is not whether "intermediaries" will benefit, but how "efficient" each form of subsidy is in relation to alternative forms. In theory, the "efficiency" of a subsidy can be measured by computing the reduction in occupancy costs it achieves as a percentage of the total subsidy costs borne by the taxpayers. The greater the "efficiency" of a subsidy, the larger the ultimate benefit provided to occupants per dollar of public funds spent.

In practice, it has proved impossible to develop any relatively simple measure of such efficiency useful in comparing all feasible forms of subsidies. "Efficiency ratios" for any given subsidy vary too much in different circumstances, and depend upon complex assumptions subject to dispute.

- Some critics of excessive ' intermediary" costs favor a housing allowance paid to occupants because then no public officials would be engaged in building and managing housing. This would appear to eliminate many expensive and inefficient administrative costs in present programs.

  a. However, a housing allowance would also require significant administrative costs. The Urban Institute has estimated that a nationwide housing allowance program would cost from $50 to $60 per household per year to administer, or from $650 to $950 million per year altogether, depending upon the number of recipients. This estimate does not include any allowance for monitoring housing quality—which would add greatly to the total cost.[12]

  b. The housing services provided by some public "intermediaries" are of great benefit to those low-income households unfamiliar with housing markets, or unable to engage in effective search and bargaining on their own. Many would not be able to meet their own housing needs effectively if required to find and bargain for housing units without such assistance. We believe counseling services should be expanded.

  c. At present, publicly built and administered housing is used by society as a means of providing shelter to many very poor, large, multi-problem households whose needs the private market refuses to meet except in extremely dilapidated units. Private owner-operators of decent quality housing consider these households too "undesirable" or "destructive" to be acceptable tenants, even when they have sufficient funds to pay prevailing rents. At least some publicly owned and operated housing is therefore required to accommodate these households—who number many thousands in large cities—if they are to occupy reasonably decent quality dwellings.

  d. We believe it would be desirable to provide a significant number of households needing housing assistance with an opportunity to do their own searching and bargaining, at least on an experimental basis. That is one reason we recommended large-scale demonstrations of housing allowances earlier in this chapter. However, we do not believe a modern industrialized society can totally eliminate the need for publicly owned and operated housing for certain large-sized groups unable to obtain decent quality housing in private markets.

- Another factor relevant to this issue is that achieving many of the basic purposes of housing subsidies other than aiding low- and moderate-income households requires action by "intermediaries." Examples are adding to the nation's supply of decent housing units, raising activity levels in the construction industry, and encouraging maximum participation in housing activities by private capital and enterprise. No housing subsidy can achieve these objectives without providing some benefits to "intermediaries" as incentives for them to carry out the desired behavior.

5. *Even if the nation fully met its official housing goal of 26 million additional units by 1978, including six million directly subsidized units, less than half of the households legally eligible for directly subsidized housing would then be living in such units. Why should we incur this tremendous cost for a program that fails to treat people in the same circumstances equally? Isn't there some more equitable way to meet the nation's housing needs?*

- The first statement in this criticism is factually correct, but somewhat misleading. The present discrepancy between legal eligibility and program coverage is actually much larger than 50 percent. In 1970, 5.2 million families and 5.0 million unrelated individuals were officially classified as "poor." It is likely that all of them—plus many more moderate-income households—were legally eligible for one or more form of direct housing subsidy. Yet the total number of directly subsidized housing units ever built in the United States was 1.85 million at the end of 1970. So the total number of legally eligible households exceeded the total number of such units by at least a five-to-one ratio. Nevertheless, not all households who are legally eligible for direct housing assistance really need it.

  a. Many elderly households with very low incomes own their own homes. They need higher incomes, not better housing. There were about 5.1 million elderly poor persons—2.55 million households—in 1970. If 50 percent of these households owned their own homes, that would mean that 1.275 million households were eligible for housing assistance but really did not need it.

  b. Most subsidized housing units are designed for households of two persons or more, not for unrelated individuals. Yet almost half of the poor households in 1970 consisted of 5.0 million unrelated individuals (including many of the elderly just discussed). Undoubtedly, the housing needs of most such persons would also be met best through higher incomes rather than housing-tied aid.

  c. Several million poor households are already receiving welfare rent allowances. Many still live in substandard dwellings, but many others have adequate quarters but inadequate incomes.

- The above facts are important in evaluating the true meaning of the enormous discrepancy between legal eligibility and planned program coverage for direct housing subsidies as of 1978. They show that this discrepancy reflects the fundamental difference between *financial* housing needs and *physical* housing needs described earlier. Present programs are designed to meet the nation's *physical* housing needs as of 1978. But the criteria for eligibility under most direct subsidy programs are based upon whether a household exhibits *financial* housing needs. As pointed out earlier, there are at least twice as many households with financial housing needs as with physical housing needs. So it is not surprising that a program designed to meet the latter will not eliminate the low incomes that cause the former.

- Is this failure really a "fault" in present programs? There can be no doubt that they now result—and will continue to result—in what looks like unequal treatment of households with equal incomes and other criteria of eligibility. That is because the designers of present housing programs looked at housing needs primarily in physical terms. Apparently they believed that any household now living in a physically sound and adequate housing unit did not need housing assistance, regardless of its income. If that income was so low that the cost of living in such good housing absorbed a high fraction of it, then the household needed more income—not better housing.

Present housing subsidy programs thus assume that if enough decent housing is built to provide physically adequate shelter for every American household, that will effectively meet the nation's housing needs. They leave it up to other policies to deal with the nation's income deficiencies. Yet income-oriented criteria are used to determine eligibility for subsidized housing so as to provide at least some new decent units directly to those now living in the worst housing. This employment of income-oriented criteria is therefore not an attempt to solve the entire low-income problem.

- In our judgment, the nation needs two different kinds of policies in this area: one type to improve the incomes of those who are poor, and another type to expand the supply of decent quality housing units— while still making good use of the huge inventory of existing housing. Those two types of policy will inevitably overlap somewhat. We do not believe that every low-income household automatically has a "housing problem" because of its poverty, regardless of the quality of its home. Yet that is precisely what conceiving of "housing needs" entirely or even mainly as *financial* housing needs really means. Hence, that is the basic implication of this criticism.

- Resolving this issue is a matter of judgment. Some people look at a poor household paying a high fraction of its income to live in a decent dwelling unit and see a poverty problem; others see a housing problem. We see a dual need to expand income maintenance and improvement programs substantially on the demand side of the market, and to expand housing production on the supply side. The latter is necessary in part to keep the demand side expansion from escalating prices, as it did so drastically concerning medical care. This issue is discussed further in later chapters.

6.   *Housing scandals have recently been uncovered in many older central-city neighborhoods. Unscrupulous real estate operators bought rundown older homes cheaply, performed "cosmetic" rehabilitation on them, obtained inflated appraisals from FHA, and sold these still-dilapidated units to unwary low-income and moderate-income households through FHA financing. The unsuspecting buyers soon discovered they needed to make costly repairs that they could not afford; so many had to default. Weren't housing subsidies basically responsible for this mess? Doesn't it prove that low-income households shouldn't be encouraged to own homes, because they basically cannot afford the operating costs? Why should the public pay for subsidies that enable crooks to exploit the poor?*

- A significant number of such scandals have occurred in several cities, notably Philadelphia, Chicago, and Detroit. The evidence does not support the charge that these scandals were caused by, or even primarily involved, the two major direct housing subsidy programs—Section 235 and Section 236. However, several lesser used housing subsidies were involved in some cases.

  a. Most of the scandals involved FHA market interest rate mortgage insurance programs, such as Section 203 (b) and Section 221 (d)(2) (a low down-payment program). The high debt service costs of these market rate programs were actually a key factor in causing households to default. In contrast, relatively low debt service costs of Section 235 units have enabled most purchasers of such units to keep up their payments. Hence, very low percentages of all defaults and default terminations in these areas have involved Section 235 units, as pointed out earlier.

  b. *Many of the units involved in scandals were insured under two programs— Section 223 and Section 237.* They provide high risk insurance for other programs, and therefore allow FHA to guarantee loans made to persons who do not qualify under normal credit rules, or who live in low quality neighborhoods. These programs encouraged FHA to insure many Section 221 (d)(2) low down-payment loans that would otherwise not have been made. Such loans formed a large share of all inner-city defaults.

- We believe there were four main causes of these scandals: deteriorating neighborhoods neglected by society, unscrupulous private real estate operators and appraisers, unwary home buyers inexperienced in real estate transactions, and poor administrative practices by FHA. Direct housing subsidies were seldom involved, as noted above, so they can hardly be considered a major cause of the defaults. Nor can their involvement be considered a condemnation of the nature of those subsidies. However, the scandals do indicate that more thorough application of the existing administrative rules is warranted, and minimum income limits should be observed in FHA programs.

a. There is no way to invest capital in deteriorating low-income neighborhoods without encountering unusually high risks in the form of high repossession rates, abandonment, vandalism, and other conditions endemic to such areas. Most private capital has stopped entering such areas to avoid these conditions. It should not be surprising, therefore, that the deliberate policy of public investment in these areas pushed by high level HUD and FHA officials after the Detroit racial disorders should result in high losses.

b. Whether such investment is warranted at all, or whether society should simply withdraw all capital from such areas, is discussed in chapter 6.

c. The possibility of dishonest and unscrupulous operation is present in all government programs. However, it is especially facilitated by inner-city real estate transactions because of their complexity, and the ignorance and naivete of many first-time home buyers.

The "Let the buyer beware" attitude of many FHA personnel working on central-city loans was totally unsuited to the circumstances. FHA should have foreseen the need for extensive counseling of new home buyers both before and after transactions. It should also have promulgated the fact that FHA financing was no guarantee of unit quality or of the seller's liability for future repairs.

d. The basic causes of FHA's inadequate administrative practices were set forth earlier. Many steps have already been taken by HUD to improve these practices and insure more thorough compliance with existing rules and regulations.

• We believe there is a real danger of both HUD and FHA overreacting to recent scandals and inner-city default rates by returning to practices of overly delayed processing times and wholly negative attitudes toward inner-city areas. It would be extremely unfortunate if the inescapable risks recently encountered in trying to deal with the tough problems of central cities were to choke off the very significant progress HUD has made in accelerating subsidized housing production since 1968, and in assisting nonaffluent households in older neighborhoods.

a. We have a strong impression that anxiety to avoid scandal has already produced a marked and possibly excessive slowdown in FHA processing in many area offices.

b. It is also our impression that a perverse incentive structure is now operating within FHA to some extent. Those area offices and officials who made the most zealous efforts to aid inner-city areas naturally encountered the highest foreclosures; whereas those who did little or nothing to aid the poor had low foreclosures. The latter are now being praised for their "prudent foresight" while the former are often chastised. We believe many of the most active offices should have exercised more foresight. But we also believe higher risks are unavoidable if society is to grapple meaningfully with inner-city problems.

  c. Overreaction is reflected in recent suggestions that FHA be made a semi-private separate agency outside HUD responsible only for non-subsidized mortgage operations.

- We strongly oppose such a separation. FHA's nonsubsidized operations are profitable, and those profits should be used to help finance activities that aid the most needy households, not to enrich private stockholders. This would be one part of the vital linkage of suburban economic growth opportunities with central-city needs.

- Moreover, such a separation would be yet another example of society's unwillingness to confront inner-city problems directly. It would exemplify the escapist tendency to flee from such problems because they are difficult to cope with and do not fit the "normal" patterns of free enterprise markets.

- Relatively high default rates and many cases of scandalous over-appraisal should not distract attention from the fact that thousands of nonaffluent households—including the majority of those who used FHA insurance in these areas—have successfully purchased their own homes because of the special risk provisions of Sections 223 and 237. Hence, these quasi-subsidy programs have at least partly accomplished their basic objective.

  a. It seems rather short-sighted to accuse policies deliberately designed to operate in high-risk situations of encountering unusually high losses. This essentially ignores the purpose of the programs.

  b. We agree that very low-income households should not be encouraged to undertake homeownership, particularly of older homes that require costly maintenance and repairs. The Section 235 program does not aim at low-income households, but at moderate-income ones. However, we believe some minimum income limits should be established to insure that all households using this program can meet the required expenses. HUD has already put such limits into effect.

  c. On the other hand, we have encountered striking evidence in even the worst quality neighborhoods that many homeowner-occupants invest extraordinary energy, resources, and labor in keeping their own dwellings in good condition—far better than the average absentee-owned buildings. This can be seen simply by driving down the streets of neighborhoods where abandonment is unusually high among larger apartments, but many smaller homes are still freshly painted and well maintained. On the basis of such evidence, we believe there is still significant validity in the theory that homeowner-occupancy motivates better maintenance and better attitudes towards property than rental tenure or absentee ownership.

7. *Aren't housing subsidies inflationary regarding construction costs? Agricultural price supports have long been capitalized into higher farm land prices; won't that happen in urban areas too if major housing subsidies are used there? Isn't it wasteful to dissipate public funds in pushing up building costs and housing prices, as we did concerning medical care?*

● Subsidizing any particular economic sector relative to others is likely to increase the amount of resources that flow into that sector. This will eventually increase the demand for whatever is produced in that sector. That will raise the costs of production, unless there are major economies of scale. Not many such economies exist regarding housing. So it is fundamentally correct to argue that larger housing subsidies will generate higher housing construction costs, if all other factors remain the same.

● However, there is no way to avoid this outcome without reducing the amount of housing produced in society. Higher demand for housing resulting from *any* cause—such as a housing allowance, or an increase in society's total private real income—will tend to increase costs of construction, at least in the short run.

Whether construction costs remain high in the long run depends upon general economic trends, stability of output, and the economies of scale in housing production. Since building trades unions are strongly organized and monopsonistic, they are not likely to allow declining or even stable wages unless compelled to do so by government regulations. Land prices are also not likely to decline much. However, both interest rates and lumber prices can fluctuate up and down sharply.

● Higher construction costs do not necessarily mean that housing costs in general will rise. In fact, housing subsidies could generate significant overproduction in relation to nonsubsidized demand, thereby exerting downward pressure on the prices of existing housing units—especially older ones.

a. The official federal program of building 26 million additional housing units from 1968 through 1978 actually amounts to a strategy of "flooding the market" with a surplus of housing units in relation to demand, thereby reducing the prices of older units.

b. We believe this has already happened in many inner-city areas, and is one of the underlying causes of rising building abandonment there.

c. This strategy for keeping housing costs in general from rising depends upon directing most housing subsidies into the supply side of the market first and thereby producing more output, rather than pumping money into the demand side first and waiting for supply to respond to resulting higher prices.

In contrast, nationwide use of a housing allowance as the main instrument of housing policy would increase prices of *existing housing* directly, and only later result in rising supply responsive to that price increase.

d. Thus, present housing subsidy programs differ sharply from medical care subsidy programs. Most current direct housing subsidies are designed to add to supply as much, or more, than they add to demand. In contrast, medical care subsidies were almost entirely aimed at expanding demand.

e. Essentially, higher housing construction costs and higher prices of the existing housing stock are two opposite conditions society can trade off against each other. The faster we build new housing, the higher construction costs will go—but the greater will be the resulting downward pressure of added supply upon the prices of existing housing (unless we increase demolitions just as fast). Conversely, the less new housing is built, the lower construction costs will be—but the greater the likelihood that "shortage" conditions will drive up prices of existing units.

- Anything that increases the general demand for urban space is likely to become capitalized in higher land prices. The only way to rapidly increase the nation's supply of decent housing without this effect is to offset it with higher taxes on land or on increases in land value.

    a. It might be desirable to accompany increased housing subsidies (as have been in effect since 1968) with increased taxes on the unearned increment of value in rising land prices. This suggests that land should be subjected to a higher capital gains tax than it is now.

    b. Another appropriate public policy reaction would be improved real property assessment practices concerning land. Vacant land is now grossly underassessed relative to other types of property in most areas.

Notes

1. The $7.8 billion represents the *maximum* annual cost of subsidies for six million units as of 1978.
2. Joint Economic Committee staff study, *The Economics of Federal Subsidy Programs* (Washington, D.C., January 11, 1972), pp. 155–156.
3. Definitions supplied by the Department of Housing and Urban Development.

4. Division of Research and Statistics, Department of Housing and Urban Development; revised February 14, 1972.

5. Subcommittee on HUD-Space-Science-Veterans, Committee on Appropriations, U.S. House of Representatives, *HUD-Space-Science-Veterans Appropriations for 1973: Hearings, Part 3, Department of Housing and Urban Development* (Washington, D.C., 1972), p. 1428.

6. Tabulation prepared by Department of Housing and Urban Development and submitted to the U.S. Senate Committee on Banking, Housing and Urban Affairs on February 29, 1972.

7. Letter to Real Estate Research Corporation from Office of the Deputy Under Secretary, Department of Housing and Urban Development, August 16, 1972.

8. *Ibid.*

9. *Ibid.*

10. *Ibid.*

11. Subcommittee of the Committee on Appropriations, U.S. House of Representatives, *HUD-Space-Science Appropriations for 1972: Hearings, Part 3, Department of Housing and Urban Development* (Washington, D.C., 1971), p. 153.

12. Sam H. Leaman, *Estimated Administrative Cost of National Housing Allowance* (Washington, D.C.: The Urban Institute Working Paper 112–17, revised February 2, 1971).

6

Alternative Overall Strategies for Coping With the Nation's Housing Needs

Basic Strategy Issues

What type of housing subsidies to use, how many units to subsidize, and who should occupy those units all depend upon what overall strategy the nation adopts regarding its housing needs. Consequently, no consideration of housing subsidies can be complete without some analysis of alternative overall strategies.

1. In the past, the nation's overall housing strategy has been arrived at almost accidentally. It has been the net result of many policy decisions made by different people without any single guiding plan. This analysis seeks to provide a framework for such a plan, or at least for understanding the implicit plans we are already following.

2. Developing such strategies is a fantastically difficult task, because housing affects everyone in society in so many different ways. We have approached this task by dividing strategy formation into seven key issues, considering each separately, then examining their interrelations. These seven issues are set forth in chart 6-1. The following sections present our main conclusions about them.

National Priorities Issue

1. A preponderant majority of American households are well housed, and are not suffering from any housing-related problems. Hence, they are not under any strong pressure to make housing a high priority national issue. In this respect, housing differs from such other issues as need for medical care, increased environmental pollution, rising property taxes, and inflation.

2. Nevertheless, for a relatively small—but absolutely large—group of Americans, inadequate housing is a critical deficiency. It is part of a cluster of deficiencies in their lives associated mainly with poverty. Creating the political support required in our majority-oriented system to help these households overcome their housing deficiencies is part of the fundamental social dilemma of removing poverty and poverty-related maladies in our society.

3. Other than poverty in general, the potentially most serious housing-related problems are those connected with deteriorating neighborhood environments in older urban areas. Adequate public policy responses to problems of neighborhood decay must involve far more comprehensive actions than

77

Chart 6-1

Basic Issues in Formulating Alternative Overall Housing Strategies

- *National Priorities Issue*
  To what extent should the creation of additional housing units, or other provision of housing-oriented aid, be given high national priority in relation to other possible use of federal funds?

- *Income Maintenance Issue*
  To what extent should we devote resources used in helping the poor to improve their physical dwelling units, as opposed to raising ther incomes so they can afford better housing, along with better everything else?

- *Spatial Location Issue*
  To what extent should we use housing subsidies to influence the spatial location of low- and moderate-income households in relation to other households? Specifically, should such subsidies be used to counteract the concentration of poverty caused by the "trickle-down" process of urban development?

- *Level of Insertion Issue*
  At what level in overall distribution of incomes should federal housing subsidies have their primary impacts? Should they concentrate upon middle- and upper-income households, moderate-income households, low-income households, or some combination of income groups?

- *Total Cost Issue*
  How much money do we want to spend on all federal housing subsidies— direct and indirect—both annually and over the next few decades?

- *Administrative Centralization Issue*
  Should there be one agency responsible for allocating federal housing subsidies to specific locations within each metropolitan area? Or should such allocation result from the separate decisions of many different builders, sponsors, consumers, and other "actors" as it does now?

- *Form-of-Subsidy Issue*
  What specific forms of housing subsidies should be used, and to what degree?

Source: Real Estate Research Corporation.

subsidies aimed at improving physical dwelling units. Yet significant amounts of housing subsidies will also be required.

4. Housing is already receiving more total public assistance than most Americans realize. Few citizens or political leaders now consider either tax deductibility benefits or housing welfare benefits as comparable to direct housing subsidies. Nevertheless, we strongly believe they are indeed comparable.

The actual distribution of all housing subsidies among income groups varies strikingly from what most Americans believe it to be. Both the middle- and upper-income groups and poor households on welfare receive more public housing-related assistance than most people realize; whereas non-welfare low-income households and all moderate-income households receive a far smaller share of all such assistance than is generally believed.

5. The present official national housing strategy involves a long-range "flood-
    ing of the market" with new housing units, as related to future increases in *filterin*
    demand. This is designed to keep prices of the existing inventory from
    rising—and to depress prices of older units so sharply that they will be
    abandoned and eventually demolished. However, we believe it will probably
    prove impossible to keep housing production at very high levels each year
    through 1978 while vacancy in the existing inventory builds up, and values
    of many existing homes are adversely affected.   *Also pop.*

    - The effectiveness of this strategy is illustrated by the fact that housing
      demolitions and other removals are now running around 700,000 units
      per year. A high fraction of these units being destroyed are probably the
      worst quality urban units.
    - Rising housing abandonment in some older central cities is also indi-
      rectly caused by expansion of alternative locations for even the poorest
      households to live.

The Income Maintenance Issue

1. Since most of the nation's *financial* housing needs arise from poverty rather
    than deficiencies in housing quality, one way to meet those needs would be
    with higher *general* income maintenance not specifically related to housing.

    - This would avoid the administrative red tape and difficulties now asso-
      ciated with housing programs. It would also provide greater freedom
      for consumers to choose their own housing and set their own spending
      patterns.
    - Some critics of present housing programs—and of other public assist-
      ance "tied" to specific commodities, such as food stamps— advocate
      such an "incomes policy" approach.

2. Categorical aid programs "tied" to specific goods or services—such as
    medical aid, food stamps, school lunch programs, and public schools—have
    several important advantages compared to "pure" income maintenance.

    - The American public is apparently willing to support greater total aid
      to the poor through several different "tied" programs than through
      direct income maintenance alone.
        a. "Tied" aid programs give weight to taxpayer preferences about how
           low-income households ought to spend assistance funds, as well as
           to the preferences of those households. Taxpayers seem more will-
           ing to support aid going to things they believe are important than
           to general income support.
        b. "Tied" aid programs also attract political support from industries
           that produce the goods or services involved.
    - An expanded nationwide income maintenance program sufficient in

scope and funding to replace existing "tied" aid programs would require a large administrative bureaucracy; hence, it might not reduce administrative costs of existing categorical programs.

- Adverse impacts upon work incentives are likely to be smaller for a set of diverse "tied" aid programs than for one large direct income maintenance program.
- Exploitation of the poor by unscrupulous operators of all types is easier when aid is provided directly in cash.
- Many objectives of "tied" aid programs are related to the specific goods or services produced, and might not result from larger income maintenance. Examples concerning housing are improving deteriorated neighborhoods, and encouraging homeownership.
- When the industry producing some specific and widely used good or service does not respond rapidly by increasing the supply available to the poor, a rise in the general purchasing power of the poor will cause rapidly rising prices if there is no easily available substitute for that good or service. Rising prices are very likely to occur concerning housing if expanded income maintenance is enacted—as experience with welfare housing allowances clearly shows. Hence, much of the aid would be dissipated in windfall benefits to landlords, rather than improved housing quality for low-income occupants.

3. Moreover, the federal government is already spending large amounts for income maintenance of various types. It spent $54.4 billion for all cash grants in fiscal 1970, and plans to spend $82.7 billion for such grants in fiscal 1973.
   - This includes retirement benefits, unemployment compensation, price supports, cash public assistance, and student aids.
   - Such spending was the equivalent of 5.7 percent of gross national product in 1970, and will be 7.0 percent in fiscal 1973.[1]

4. For the above reasons, we believe that some form of subsidy "tied" to housing should definitely be continued in the future, even if an expanded income maintenance program is adopted. However, we also believe the latter should have high priority as a means of combatting poverty in general.

5. There are two basic forms of categorical subsidies "tied" to housing: supply expansion and demand expansion.
   - *Supply expansion subsidies* tie the subsidy to creation of a new or rehabilitated housing unit, although they may also add to demand at the same time. They initially flow through the housing production industry and benefit consumers by (1) reducing the occupancy cost of those living in the new units, and (2) adding to the total supply, thereby putting downward pressure on the prices of all existing units.
     a. These subsidies require complex administration because they deal with *both* housing suppliers and housing consumers.

   b. Examples of supply expansion subsidies are the Section 235 and Section 236 programs, the conventional and turnkey public housing programs, and the rent supplement new construction program.

- *Demand expansion subsidies* tie the subsidy to a household, which then uses "normal" housing markets to meet its needs. They initially flow through consumer households, benefiting their recipients through reduced occupancy costs.

   a. These subsidies affect total housing supply indirectly by raising prices and thereby calling forth more total output in the long run (including better maintenance of existing units).

   b. These subsidies are much easier to administer than supply expansion subsidies if they do not require any periodic checks on the quality of housing occupied by the recipients. If such checks are required, they are probably almost as hard to administer as supply-oriented subsidies, though they can be put into effect faster.

   c. Examples of demand expansion subsidies are the income tax deductibility subsidy, a housing allowance paid to the occupants, and the public housing leasing subsidy applied to existing units.

- Two key factors relevant to determining which of these forms of categorical aid to housing is superior in a given situation are the degree of housing shortage for low-income households, and the likely responsiveness of the housing supply industry to greater demand by low-income households.

   a. Where there is a marked shortage of units available to low-income households and a relatively unresponsive housing supply industry, large-scale use of demand expansion subsidies will produce rapidly rising prices without much improvement in housing quality for those aided. This will injure other households not receiving the aid by raising their prices too.

   b. Where there is an ample supply of existing housing units (as indicated by relatively high vacancy or abandonment rates) but maintenance is poor because of low cash flows to owners, then demand expansion subsidies can increase effective use of the existing inventory without dissipating too much aid as rising prices.

   c. Thus, local housing market conditions should have an important influence upon which form of housing related categorical assistance is used in any specific area.

- Another important consideration in selecting which type of housing subsidy to use is that supply expansion subsidies can involve new construction of units for low- and moderate-income households; whereas demand expansion subsidies probably cannot.

   a. Congress would probably not support demand expansion housing subsidies with large enough per-unit amounts to allow low- and

Chart 6-2

Alternative Options Concerning the Location and Intensity of Future
Urban Development Activities Responsive to Public Policies and Funding

Short Title	Brief Description in Terms of Key Variables
1. Contained Decay	Continued exclusion of low- and moderate-income households from most suburbs; no large-scale investment of either income maintenance or physical improvements in inner-city decaying areas.
2. Non-Capital Enrichment Only	Continued exclusion and no large-scale investment in physical inner-city improvements, but adoption of large-scale income maintenance and related social service delivery programs.
3. All-Out Enrichment Only	Continued exclusion, but large-scale investment in both physical improvement and income maintenance and other social service delivery systems in inner-city decaying areas.
4. Decay Plus Dispersal	No major investment in inner-city areas, but adoption of major program to provide low- and moderate-income housing on sites throughout metropolitan areas outside of inner-city decaying areas.
5. Non-Capital Enrichment Plus Dispersal	Large-scale income maintenance and social service delivery programs in inner-city decaying areas, plus major dispersal programs, but no physical improvement of inner-city decaying areas.
6. Non-Capital Enrichment, Dispersal, and Delayed Physical Redevelopment	Same as (5) above, except major physical improvement programs launched in inner-city decaying areas *after* interim period while values decline there, making acquisition less costly.
7. All-Out Enrichment Plus Dispersal and as Rapid Physical Redevelopment as Possible	Combines large-scale income maintenance and social service delivery in inner-city decaying areas, major dispersal programs in remainder of metropolitan areas, and gradual physical improvement of inner-city areas launched at same time as non-capital enrichment, proceeding as fast as possible.

Source: Real Estate Research Corporation.

moderate-income households to occupy brand new units—unless
those subsidies were highly restricted to a few areas. The total cost
of making such large per-unit subsidies available to *all* income
eligible households would be too great.

b. Thus, only supply expansion subsidies can provide the five major
benefits of building new units for low- and moderate-income
households described earlier.

c. Our conclusions and recommendations concerning use of new construction-oriented subsidies vs. use of a housing allowance were set
forth in chapter 5.

The Spatial Location Issue

1. The present urban development process inherently generates major problems in older central-city neighborhoods by concentrating large numbers of low-income households there. It also separates such households from the rapidly expanding economic opportunities caused by population and economic growth in suburban areas.

   • An important aspect of any overall housing strategy is formulating and evaluating alternative means of coping with these dual deficiencies. We believe the major alternative choices facing society about *where within metropolitan areas* to invest future resources for this purpose can be summarized in terms of seven different options for locational emphasis. These are shown in chart 6-2.

   • Suburban dominance of both population and economic growth is almost sure to continue in the near future. Therefore, all seven of these options assume continued major investment of both public and private resources in all types of suburban facilities and activities.

   • The main variables among these options concern the degree to which each will involve:

     a. Large-scale income maintenance and social service delivery programs aiding inner-city residents (*non-capital enrichment*).

     b. Large-scale physical capital investment programs upgrading inner-city neighborhoods (the second ingredient in *all-out enrichment*).

     c. Major programs aimed at dispersing low- and moderate-income households throughout each metropolitan area—or at least in many locations outside areas where they are now concentrated, including suburban locations.

   • These alternatives incorporate six of the eight combinations possible if each variable is conceived of as having two potential values: yes or no. The two combinations omitted as unlikely are those calling for major physical renewal of inner-city decaying areas without any large income maintenance or social service delivery programs there.

2. We believe present policies amount to something between the *contained decay* and *non-capital enrichment only* options. Some income maintenance and social service delivery are now going into inner-city decaying areas—although not enough to be full-scale non-capital enrichment. There is also very little physical improvement there, or dispersal elsewhere.

   • Key factors to consider in deciding which of these options society should choose include the following:

     a. Continued growth of the central-city low-income population, plus more abandonment of neighborhoods in some cities, will cause a constant future expansion of urban decay in older central cities if present policies remain unchanged. Hence, "Contained Decay" really means constantly expanding decay.

b. Continued concentration of poverty in older central-city neighborhoods will undermine the effectiveness of any physical improvements made there. Thus, we believe some type of dispersal policy is essential to any long-range upgrading of the quality of life in these areas.

- Dispersal into new-growth suburban areas requires subsidies that allow low- and moderate-income occupancy of brand new units. Therefore, the greater the social policy emphasis on dispersal as part of any strategy, the more important the role of new construction-oriented housing subsidies.
- Housing subsidies alone will probably not cause much direct outward movement from inner-city poverty areas into dispersed locations without specific incentives tied to such movement.

c. Strictly voluntary dispersal of at least some low- and moderate-income households throughout each metropolitan area would provide the following benefits:

- Easier access of such households to expanding suburban job opportunities.
- Greater opportunities for such households to upgrade themselves by escaping from the destructive environment of concentrated poverty areas.
- Improved quality education for the children from such households.
- A higher probability that the nation would reach its official housing goal of six million additional subsidized units by 1978. Achievement of that goal will require building many such units on vacant suburban land.
- Fairer geographic distribution of the fiscal and social costs of dealing with metropolitan-area poverty. These costs are now disproportionately loaded onto central-city residents.
- A reduced probability that the United States will develop two separate and unequal societies within its metropolitan areas, as feared by the National Advisory Commission on Civil Disorders (the "Kerner Commission").

d. Large-scale physical improvement of inner-city decaying areas would be extremely expensive, unless it was delayed until land prices fell very low because of advanced abandonment, or some type of low-cost public acquisition process was developed.

Existing repossession laws need to be radically changed—at least as applied to certain designated decaying areas. Public authorities need to be able to occupy physically vacant units with payment delinquencies almost immediately; otherwise, vandals render them useless for shelter purposes.

e. Some new mechanism for *neighborhood management* is needed to provide for a more orderly quality of life in inner-city decaying areas—whatever future strategy is adopted toward them. These areas contain fragmented property ownership, plus very low incomes, plus very low levels of personal and physical security. As a result, social and personal problems spill over from one household or housing unit to others nearby. No local resources are available to respond with either stronger social controls or compensating investments.

- This is what causes abandonment to spread from dilapidated units that deserve to be demolished to sound units nearby that could be preserved and furnish good housing to those who need it.
- The most crucial single improvement in urban affairs would be effective local surveillance or other arrangements providing high level personal and property security in these decaying urban neighborhoods. This in turn requires radical reform in the existing system of criminal justice, which simply does not work in such areas.

3. Specific uses of housing subsidies that might encourage dispersal include spreading out subsidy allocations over more communities in each metropolitan area, tying other federal aids to acceptance of subsidized housing, providing greater counseling to inner-city households to aid them in finding dispersed housing, and creating "impact" subsidies for communities accepting low- and moderate-income households.

Level of Insertion Issue

1. Overall housing strategies can be differentiated by the *levels* in the income distribution at which they insert both new housing units and housing subsidy aids. For example, conventional public housing involves the insertion of some new units at a low level in the income distribution by focusing housing subsidies there.

2. The present overall structure of housing laws, regulations, and subsidies in the United States encourages predominantly middle- and upper-level insertion of new housing units. This occurs both because legally enforced high quality standards prohibit low-cost new units (except mobile homes), and because the largest housing subsidy—the income tax deductibility subsidy—goes mainly to middle- and upper-income homeowning households.

- It is not very likely that this built-in bias towards relatively high level insertion will be altered in the near future. Both high quality laws and the income tax deductibility subsidy are probably too popular to be significantly changed, since about 63 percent of all American households own their own homes.

- Whenever direct housing subsidies supporting low- and moderate-level insertion are at low funding levels (as was always the case until about 1965), the primary source of housing for low- and moderate-income households is the "trickle-down" process. The basic built-in bias towards middle- and upper-level insertion further reinforces the dominance of the "trickle-down" process.

  Although about 2.3 million directly subsidized housing units have been created in the United States, there were about 5.9 million households in metropolitan areas in 1970 with incomes low enough to be officially classified as "poor" (including both families and unrelated individuals). Even excluding all moderate-income households, it is therefore clear that the "trickle-down" process is still the dominant source of housing for most low-income households.

3.   The net cost/benefit "efficiency" of any housing subsidy strategy is affected by the levels of insertion it emphasizes, both directly and through the "chains of movement" generated by every new housing unit created.
   - New units inserted at relatively high levels in the income distribution start longer "chains of movement" than those inserted lower. But those chains affect a lower percentage of low- and moderate-income households.
       a. Expensive new homes start chains in which an average of as many as 3.8 households upgrade their housing. But only about ten percent of those households have low incomes—based on the sketchy data compiled on this subject to date.[2]
       b. Direct housing subsidies that cause low- and moderate-income level insertions start shorter chains—probably averaging around 2.0 households— but nearly all households involved have low and moderate incomes.
   - Traditionally, high level insertion has been considered a far less expensive method of providing housing for the relatively poor—in terms of costs to the public—than lower level insertion created by direct housing subsidies, since high level insertion appeared to have no subsidy costs. But when both indirect subsidy costs (mainly the income tax deductibility subsidy) and chains of movement are taken into account, directly subsidized lower level insertion can be just as efficient in terms of the total subsidy cost per low- and moderate-income household aided. Moreover, lower level insertion allows those households to live in brand new units rather than older ones.
   - On the other hand, middle level insertion without direct subsidies benefits more *total households* at all income levels per dollar of subsidy cost than either high level or low level insertion.
   - To illustrate these variations, we have set forth in table 6-1 some rough estimates based upon plausible assumptions about several different types

Table 6-1
Estimated Comparative Total Subsidy Costs per Household Aided by Unit Types, Taking Account of all Subsidies and Moves

| Type of New Housing Unit | Development and Construction Cost | Forms of Subsidy Involved | | Estimated Average Annual Subsidy Size Per Unit* | | Total Number of Moves** | Estimated Percentage of Moving Households with | | Total Subsidy Cost Per Household Aided | | |
		Direct	Indirect	Direct	Indirect		Low Incomes	Moderate Incomes	For all Households Aided	Low- and Moderate-Income Households Only	Low-Income Households Only
1. Section 235 New•	$21,000	Interest Reduction	Tax Deductibility	$ 731	$ 370	3.0	16.7%	83.3%	$367	$ 367	$2,202
2. Section 236 New•	$17,500	Interest Reduction	Accelerated Depreciation	$ 765	$ 127	2.0	25.0%	75.0%	$446	$ 446	$1,784
3. Section 236 New plus Rent Supplement•	$17,500	Interest Reduction and Income Aid	Accelerated Depreciation	$1,773	$ 127	2.0	100.0%	—	$950	$ 950	$ 950
4. Public Housing—Conventional plus Operating Cost Subsidy	$20,000	Debt Service Payment plus Income Aid	Reduced Property Tax	$1,316	$ 300	2.0	100.0%	—	$808	$ 808	$ 803
5. Public Housing Leasing	—	Leased Fee Payments	None	$1,056	—	2.0	100.0%	—	$528	$ 528	$ 528
6. Non-Directly—Subsidized Unit, New and Owner-Occupied	$24,000	None	Tax Deductibility	—	$ 326	3.0	10.0%	25.0%	$109	$ 310	$1,087
7. Same as above	$33,000	None	Tax Deductibility	—	$ 573	3.8	10.0%	26.3%	$151	$ 415	$1,508
8. Same as above	$60,000	None	Tax Deductibility	—	$1,629	3.5	10.0%	28.6%	$465	$1,206	$4,654

•Maximum interest subsidy assumed.
*Average per year over first seven years.
**Including household moving into new unit.
Sources: Real Estate Research Corporation; movement chain data drawn from several studies.

of housing units inserted at different levels, taking into account all subsidies and chains of movements.

4. We have formulated seven alternative options concerning the appropriate mixture of income maintenance and housing production choices, with variations concerning the following key variables:
   - The relative emphasis placed upon "pure" income maintenance, demand-expanding housing subsidies (presumably some type of housing allowance), and supply-expanding housing subsidies (especially those involving new construction).
   - The levels of insertion where most new housing units are placed.
   These seven strategy choices are depicted in chart 6–3.

5. These choices represent only seven of the twelve logically possible combinations if income maintenance and housing allowances are each conceived of as having two potential values (yes or no) and housing construction three values (high level only, high level plus some at other levels, or high level plus large amounts at other levels). Most of the five combinations we omitted seem implausible because they involve no income maintenance.

   All seven choices are assumed to continue major emphasis upon high level insertion of new units because of the built-in bias described above.

6. We believe the present situation in the United States could most accurately be characterized as lying somewhere between options five and six. It is marked by large-scale insertion of new units at all levels, with both indirect and direct subsidies, relatively modest income maintenance, and no housing allowance program per se (although several existing subsidies have some of the qualities of a housing allowance).

7. Key factors to consider in deciding which of these options society should choose include the following:
   - Experience indicates that sole reliance upon the "trickle-down" process to provide adequate housing for the poor does not produce satisfactory results. It generates excessive concentrations of poverty in older inner-city areas, and takes too long to get housing down to the poorest households.
   - Experience also indicates that combatting poverty through programs that isolate assistance to the poor from assistance to more affluent citizens usually causes Congress to hold down the assistance to the poor—even though they need it most. This indicates that income maintenance alone may not be an adequate anti-poverty weapon.
   - Major stimulation of the demand for housing at low- and moderate-income levels through either income maintenance or housing allowances could produce excessive increases in housing prices and rents if not accompanied by a significant amount of new construction inserted at those same levels.

Chart 6-3

Alternative Options Concerning the Proper Mixture of Income
Maintenance and Housing Subsidies, Types of Housing Subsidies,
and the Levels of Their Insertion

Short Title	Brief Description
1. "Trickle-Down" Plus Minimal Anti-Poverty	High level insertion with only tax deductibility subsidies, complete reliance on "trickle-down" to house poor, very little income maintenance directly to poor.
2. Pure Anti-Poverty	High level housing insertion as in (1) above, but massive income maintenance to poor at bottom of the income distribution.
3. Accelerated "Trickle-Down"	Maximized high level insertion with "normal" quantities of housing units produced, augmented by favorable monetary and fiscal policies; *both* large-scale income maintenance and a large-scale housing allowance program to counteract poverty; no low level insertion of *new* directly subsidized housing.
4. Accelerated "Trickle-Down" Marginally Augmented	Same as (3), but with *some* insertion of *new* directly subsidized housing to achieve limited dispersal and other objectives best served by such new construction.
5. All-Out New Construction With Minimal Anti-Poverty	Large-scale insertion of new housing at all levels similar to (6), but very little emphasis upon income maintenance, and no housing allowance.
6. All-Out New Construction Plus Anti-Poverty	*Large-scale* insertion of *new* housing units at *all* levels (high, middle, moderate, and low) through relevant indirect and direct subsidies. No housing allowance, but big income maintenance.
7. Mixed Options	Significant insertion of new housing units at all levels using appropriate subsidies though less massive than in (6) above. Income maintenance at significant scale, plus some use of housing allowance, but not on nationwide basis.

Source: Real Estate Research Corporation.

- The factors cited above indicate that Options 1, 2, and 3 on chart 6-3
  ("Trickle-Down" Plus Minimal Anti-Poverty, Pure Anti-Poverty, and
  Accelerated "Trickle-Down") are not very desirable.

The Total Cost Issue

1. Current housing subsidy programs involve very large annual expenditures as
   well as legally enforceable long-term commitments to future spending over

as many as forty years. How much should the nation spend on these or other housing-related programs?

- This broad question can best be considered by examining six specific issues, which are set forth in chart 6-4 as additional questions.
- The results of our efforts to answer these questions are presented below.

2. We believe future costs of housing subsidy programs and all other programs should be discounted before being compared with present dollars or with other future costs. This is consistent both with prevailing investment practices in the private sector and with congressional tendencies to weight near-future benefits more heavily than distant-future costs.

- The reality of congressional discounting is illustrated by the use of interest reduction subsidies rather than capital grants. The $624 per year rent saving from the interest reduction subsidy on a $17,000 Section 236 unit has a "lifetime" cost of $24,978 if the maximum subsidy lasts for forty years. The same reduction in rents could be produced by an initial $9,092 capital grant with a market rate mortgage for the remaining cost—or a "lifetime"subsidy cost only 36 percent as large. However, the interest rate reduction subsidy produces far more units *immediately* per million dollars spent: 1,602 vs. 110 for capital grants. Although the capital grant approach would *eventually* produce more units over forty years of one-million-dollars-per-year spending (4,400 vs. 1,602), it would take 14.5 years to build as many units as the interest rate subsidy provided in the first year. Congress has consistently rejected the capital grant approach in favor of interest reduction subsidies because Congress implicitly discounts future costs and benefits in relation to present ones—as we believe it should. Capital grants also produce a much larger immediate budgetary impact per unit than interest reduction subsidies, but that is another way of saying the same thing as above.
- Simply "running out" program costs over forty years, and then adding up the results without discounting, produces estimates of future costs (or benefits) that are mistakenly perceived as equivalent in importance and probability of occurrence to the same number of current dollars. This causes false impressions about the real costs involved. It tends to create "alarmist" views of housing programs as compared to other programs for which no such future estimates are made.

  Almost all significant programs have alarming sounding total costs if their present annual levels are projected forward over forty years and then added without discounting. For example, table 6-2 shows the total forty-year cost of various federal programs calculated as though their annual levels remained exactly the same as in 1972 for the next forty years. Because inflation will raise those annual levels in the future,

Chart 6-4

Key Questions Regarding the Total Amount That the Nation
"Ought to" Spend on Housing and Housing Subsidies

- Should future dollars be discounted before being compared with present dollars?

- Is the important cost the one that enters the federal budget, or the one that measures the total amount of resources actually consumed by housing?

- Is the important cost the annual level of spending, or the total lifetime amount, or some other measure?

- Can total lifetime costs be accurately forecast for programs that have many variable-cost features and last up to forty years?

- Is future spending that is required by contractual arrangements of greater significance than future spending that is likely to occur but is not contractually required?

- With what should total spending on housing subsidies, however calculated, be compared to determine whether it is a large or small amount? Should it be compared to gross national product, or the federal budget, or specific subsidies for other activities, or what?

the forty-year totals will actually be much larger than the figures in table 6-2.

- Discounting also allows more meaningful comparisons of programs with very different future timing of costs and benefits.

- It is not clear whether the most appropriate discount rate is (1) the federal borrowing rate, (2) the marginal private rate of return representing what taxpayers sacrifice, or (3) the ten percent calculation rate now required by the Office of Management and Budget (when discounting is used). We believe the last rate is too high and suggest calculations using both the first two for comparison.

3. Costs that do not appear in the federal budget directly—but still must be paid by taxpayers— should certainly be included in calculating total subsidy costs. Moreover, it is desirable to distinguish between *income transfers*

Table 6-2

Projected 40-Year Costs of Selected Federal Nonhousing Programs

Program	1972 Annual Spending— Billions	Projected 40-Year Total at That Level— Billions
Defense	$75.8	$3,032.0
Net Interest on Debt	$14.4	$ 576.0
Medicare and Medicaid	$12.4	$ 496.0

Sources: Real Estate Research Corporation projections.

Table 6–3
Percentage of Gross National Product Spent on Housing
Between 1956 and 1966 in Six Nations

Nation	Highest Year	Lowest Year
United States	5.5%	3.4%
West Germany	5.9%	4.8%
Sweden	5.9%	5.1%
Netherlands	5.2%	3.8%
France	6.7%	4.3%
United Kingdom	3.7%	2.8%

Source: Howard R. Moskof, "Foreign Housing Subsidy Systems: Alternative Approaches," paper submitted to Subcommittee on Housing Panels, House Committee on Banking and Currency, 92nd Congress.

and *real consumption of resources* in certain types of calculations (although we have not done so in this study).

- We believe it would be extremely misleading to ignore non-budgetary subsidy costs, especially since they form nearly two-thirds of all housing subsidy costs.
- When a new Section 236 unit costing $17,500 is built, the total *subsidy cost* is $892 per year (including both interest rate reduction and accelerated depreciation subsidies), but the total *resource cost* of creating the unit is $17,500. We believe both types of cost should be taken into account, but for different purposes.
  a. The total resource cost should be used in determining whether sufficient capital is available to meet programed production, what the employment effects will be, and whether reaching any specific production target is likely to produce inflationary impacts.
  b. The subsidy cost should be considered when weighing the cost of alternative subsidy programs to achieve a given housing production goal. However, most subsidies represent income transfers from one group to another, rather than real absorptions of resources.
  c. Since this study is mainly about housing subsidies, we focus primarily upon subsidy costs in most of our analysis.

4. Both annual and "lifetime" costs should be considered in making housing subsidy decisions. However, it is very difficult to forecast "lifetime" costs of many current federal housing subsidies, and a proposed housing allowance, because of uncertainties inherent in their design.

Many current federal subsidies, and others proposed, are income "gap"-tied, as discussed earlier. Their future size depends upon how fast consumer incomes rise in relation to housing costs. Yet both are difficult to forecast as far ahead as the thirty to forty years for which legal commitments are made in these programs.

5.   We believe it is unrealistic to regard contractual commitments for future spending as somehow more binding than noncontractual commitments which, once made, would be extremely difficult to eliminate for political reasons. For example, once a nationwide housing allowance program was adopted, it would be very difficult politically to halt it—even though no contractual commitments beyond one year would be involved. Hence, it is just as important to examine future costs of such a program over a long period as it is to examine those contractually required by mortgage loans.

6.   How much public money a nation "ought to" spend on housing and housing subsidies altogether is a relative question. The answer depends in part upon its general standard of living, the importance of housing in the lives of citizens, and what it is spending on other activities or services of comparable importance. Perspective on this question is best obtained by making several different comparisons, as shown below.

- Regarding total resource costs expended on housing, the share of gross national product devoted to housing in the recent past has not been as large as in earlier parts of the post-World War II period. The highest modern share of GNP devoted to housing was 5.5 percent in 1950. From 1965 through 1971, the share ranged from a low of 3.2 percent (in 1967) to a high of 4.1 percent (in 1965 and 1971).

- Other industrialized nations spend as much or more of their gross national product on housing as the United States. Fractions of gross national product spent on housing in the highest-fraction and lowest-fraction years from 1956 to 1966 for six industrialized nations are shown in table 6-3.

- The capital resources required to meet present national housing goals could be supplied without placing an excessive strain on the economy. The *Second Annual Report on National Housing Goals* estimates that the total non-land capital could be supplied by devoting a maximum of 4.3 percent of gross national product to housing in the period from 1970 through 1978, and only 3.79 percent in 1978. This is more than the average in recent years, but far less than the postwar high in 1950.

  a. Determining whether the other resources required—such as labor, construction materials, and land—could be supplied without inflationary effects is beyond the scope of this study.

  b. However, it is our general opinion that national housing goals could be met if housing were given an even higher national priority than it has now, and if the economy did not operate at full employment most of the time between now and 1978 (since full employment conditions tend to divert capital away from housing and cause rapidly rising housing costs).

7.   Comparison of federal housing subsidies with other federal subsidies provides useful perspective concerning how much should be spent on housing

Table 6–4
Total Federal Subsidy Costs, Fiscal 1970
(In billions of dollars)

Area of Activity	Cash Payment Subsidies	Tax Subsidies	Credit Subsidies	In-kind Subsidies	Total Subsidies
1. Agriculture	$ 3.879	$ 0.880	$ 0.443	–	$ 5.202
2. Medical Care	$ 0.973	$ 3.150	$ 0.052	$ 4.617	$ 8.792
3. Manpower	$ 1.991	$ 0.550	–	–	$ 2.541
4. Education	$ 1.976	$ 0.785	$ 0.434	$ 0.409	$ 3.604
5. International Trade	$ 0.106	$ 0.420	$ 0.623	$ 0.034	$ 1.183
6. *Housing*	$ 0.195[1]	$ 5.680[2]	$ 2.550[4]	–	$ 8.425
7. Natural Resources	$ 0.330	$ 1.970	$ 0.022	$ 0.712	$ 3.034
8. Transportation	$ 0.300	$ 0.010	–	$ 0.362	$ 0.672
9. Commerce and Economic Development	$ 2.051	$15.635[3]	$ 0.059	$ 1.518	$19.263
10. Other	–	$ 9.400 (Misc.)	–	$ 1.593 (Food)	$10.993
Total	$11.801	$38.480	$ 4.183	$ 9.245	$63.709

1. Includes rent supplement payments, which are expressed in capitalized value and total $163 million; rehabilitation grants; farm labor housing grants; and special housing for disabled veterans.

2. Does *not* include estimate of imputed net rent. Does include deductibility of interest and property taxes on owner-occupied homes; accelerated depreciation on rental housing; and five-year write-off of rehabilitation costs for low-income housing.

3. Includes estimates of corporate capital gains other than agriculture and natural resources, taken separately; estimate of accelerated depreciation revision not available and not included.

4. Includes following programs, which are guaranteed or insured loans, debt service payments, or combination of the two: Section 235, Section 236, Section 221(d)(3) BMIR, rural housing insurance, low rent public housing.

Source: *The Economics of Federal Subsidy Programs,* A Staff Study prepared for the Joint Economic Committee, Congress of the United States, January 11, 1972.

subsidies. Table 6–4 sets forth estimates of all federal subsidies for fiscal 1970 made by the staff of the Joint Economic Committee of Congress in its report, *The Economics of Federal Subsidy Programs,* dated January 11, 1972.

- Table 6–4 includes interest reduction subsidies (like Section 235) on a capitalized basis, and omits "excess costs" of services provided to users at less than full cost (a minor amount).
- According to these data, total federal subsidies in fiscal 1970 were $63.7 billion, equivalent to around 6.5 percent of gross national product. They equaled about one-third of all federal expenditures in that year, although many of these subsidies were not in the budget.
- Housing subsidies totaled $8.4 billion, or 13 percent of all federal sub-

Table 6–5

Ranking of Federal Subsidies by Area of Activity

Area of Activity	Total Direct and Indirect Subsidies	Percentage of All Federal Subsidies	Ratio to Housing Subsidies
	(Billions)		
1. Commerce and Economic Development	$19.263	30.2%	2.29
2. Medical Care	$ 8.792	13.8%	1.04
3. *Housing*	$ 8.425	13.2%	1.00
4. Agriculture	$ 5.202	8.2%	.62
5. Education	$ 3.604	5.7%	.43
6. Natural Resources	$ 3.034	4.8%	.36
7. Manpower	$ 2.541	4.0%	.30
8. International Trade	$ 1.183	1.9%	.14
9. Transportation	$ 0.672	1.1%	.08

Source: *The Economics of Federal Subsidy Programs.*

sidies. This does not include welfare rent allowances, which were not defined as subsidies in this study. Their inclusion would bring the total close to $11 billion, or more than one percent of gross national product.

- Housing ranked third among major areas of activity in total size of federal subsidies provided, behind commerce plus economic development and medical care. A ranking of all types of subsidies (except "other") is shown in table 6–5.

- Housing subsidies are now much larger than most people realize. They are usually calculated from annual budgetary expenditures, which omit almost two-thirds of the total.

- Data for fiscal 1971 confirm all the above conclusions, but were not quite as complete as those for fiscal 1970.

The Administrative Centralization Issue

1. Current federal housing subsidy programs have been criticized because subsidized units are located not in accordance with a single overall plan, but in response to the separate initiatives of thousands of individual builders and sponsors. This does not result in a clearly rational and effective geographic pattern of subsidized housing placement in each metropolitan area, related to its specific needs.

- Consequently, recent proposed legislation calls for transferring subsidy allocation power to a single housing agency with metropolitan-wide jurisdiction in each metropolitan area, or a state agency with jurisdiction outside of metropolitan areas.

- Theoretically, such centralized administration over subsidy allocations would allow development and implementation of a single, comprehensive pattern of placement much more effective than present practices in meeting each area's real needs.

2. To achieve this goal, such an areawide agency would have to meet six conditions simultaneously. It would have to be:

- Able to place subsidized units within any local community in the area, regardless of whether or not the community's government or citizens approved, so long as those units met prevailing codes and zoning rules.
- Free from political domination by those interests wanting to prevent widespread location of low- and moderate-income housing throughout the area. In most areas, these interests probably include a majority of all residents.
- Run by leaders dedicated to the creation of a large amount of low- and moderate-income housing, and willing to take the initiative to see that it is built, regardless of how popular or unpopular taking that stand made them.
- Not likely to be paralyzed by indecision resulting from conflicts of values or goals among different groups within the area.
- Not likely to become bogged down in administrative delays.
- Capable of developing comprehensive plans for meeting the housing needs of the entire area.

3. It is extremely unlikely that any areawide agency with even mildly effective political connections to existing local governments would be able to meet most of these conditions. Yet Congress is not likely to set up areawide agencies that are unrelated to existing local governments within each metropolitan area.

- The main difficulty that areawide agencies would have is that most suburban governments and residents are opposed to placement of subsidized housing for low- and moderate-income households in their communities. Yet suburbanites constitute a majority in most metropolitan areas.
    a. Hence, the more politically responsive to the areas' constituents comprehensive agencies became, the less able they would be to place subsidized housing in their communities.
    b. Yet, in our opinion, a crucial ingredient in any effective areawide plan would be major dispersal of low- and moderate-income housing to nearly all parts of the area. The suburban majority would probably oppose such dispersal strongly, or at least attach to it so many restrictions as to make it ineffective.

4. The present decentralized administration strategy of leaving the initiative to individual builders and sponsors actually meets five of the six conditions set forth above better than an areawide agency would. Its one deficiency is that it is incapable of developing a single comprehensive plan responsive to an area's needs.

- The initiative of individual builders and sponsors is far less susceptible to being stopped by the political sentiments of a community than that of officials in an areawide agency controlling allocations—especially one that has political ties to existing governments.

- HUD can impose a certain degree of comprehensiveness and rationality on the existing system by using standardized locational criteria—as it has recently begun to do. Since HUD area-office administrators are not directly elected or directly linked to local government officials, they are actually more likely to impose certain criteria upon reluctant communities than officials in an areawide agency would be, under most circumstances.

- The effectiveness of the current system would be further improved by reductions in the ability of individual communities to exclude subsidized housing through manipulation of building codes and zoning ordinances. Hence, HUD should press for statewide codes and reasonable nonexclusionary zoning (as has been done in part through Operation Breakthrough).

  If local communities could be "disarmed" in their ability to exclude directly subsidized housing, and HUD employed site selection criteria responsive to areawide needs and to the location of all other subsidized units, the current system could even approach development of an implicit comprehensive plan.

5. We believe that under present political conditions, the existing decentralized administrative strategy—augmented as described above by HUD policies —would probably result in more effective areawide placement of directly subsidized housing than the proposed centralized administrative strategy, at least in most areas.

   However, sufficient uncertainty about this matter exists to warrant conducting several experiments or demonstrations involving areawide allocation agencies in specific metropolitan areas. We recommend initiation of five to ten such experiments as soon as possible. We believe this would be a far more sensible approach than immediately switching to such an untried mechanism nationwide. Moreover, this approach is consistent with the Administration's previous experimental approach to such major new policy mechanisms as the negative income tax and a housing allowance.

The Form-of-Subsidies Issue

1. In relation to overall housing strategy, which subsidy forms to use depends upon what characteristics are required to achieve the objectives of the basic strategy options chosen.

- Regarding *spatial strategy* options:
  a. *Dispersal strategies* require at least some new construction-oriented subsidies that insert new units at low- and moderate-income levels. However, subsidies that allow more intensive use of the existing inventory could aid dispersal in older suburban and central-city peripheral areas with substantial vacancies.
  b. *Non-dispersal strategies* indicate greater emphasis upon a housing allowance or other subsidies calling for more intensive use of the existing inventory. However, they also require new construction-oriented subsidies when vacancy rates in the older inventory are low in poor areas.
  c. *Physical redevelopment strategies* that emphasize rebuilding inner-city decaying areas would require a mixture of both of the subsidy types discussed above.
- Regarding *level of insertion strategy* options, the main alternatives are relatively self-explanatory in relation to subsidy forms. High-level insertion is aided by the income tax deductibility subsidy and accelerated depreciation. Low- and moderate-level insertions require direct subsidies that finance new construction of units for those income groups. The degree of emphasis upon a housing allowance is also part of the definition of each strategy option.

2. It is not necessary to analyze the relationship between strategy options and the subsidy forms appropriate to each option in much more detail. The implications for subsidy forms of each strategy option can be rather easily developed once the options considered most desirable have been chosen.

Putting It All Together

1. It is apparent from the preceding analysis that choosing an overall housing strategy is an extraordinarily complicated task. We have attempted to approach that task by considering a number of strategic issues separately. The specific findings and conclusions derived from considering each issue can be applied to whatever choice is made among the many different options set forth concerning both the *spatial* and *level of insertion* aspects of an overall strategy.

2. However, in order to illuminate the real choices among those options further, we have combined the seven spatial strategy options and the seven level of insertion strategy options into one "grand strategy" matrix. This matrix is presented in chart 6-5.
   - The purpose of this seemingly esoteric exercise is to narrow down the many theoretical possible combinations of these two types of options to a manageable number. Hopefully, the number will be small enough to

provide a clearer insight into the types of choices that society really could make concerning its overall housing strategy. This, in turn, will allow clearer analysis of the possible consequences of each such choice, and provide useful guidance to those who must make that choice—or contribute to making it.

- The Grand Strategy Matrix has Level of Insertion and Income Maintenance Options as columns, and Spatial Development Emphasis and Income Maintenance Options as rows. The result is forty-nine squares, each representing a logically possible combination of options.

- However, not all forty-nine logically possible combinations represent practically consistent situations. In many cases, the characteristics of the Spatial Development Emphasis and Income Maintenance Option are incompatible with those of the Level of Insertion and Income Maintenance Option. The precise nature of these inconsistencies is spelled out in nine "Elimination Rules" shown at the right side of the chart. Each of the eliminated squares contains the numbers of the rules that describe its internal inconsistency.

  a. In fact, these rules eliminate thirty-six of the forty-nine logically possible combinations—leaving only thirteen that represent practically feasible combinations of these two different types of options.

  b. The thirteen feasible combinations are outlined heavily and printed in red, and some have been given brief titles to indicate their nature.

3. The following significant conclusions can be drawn from an analysis of this Grand Strategy Matrix:

- There is a strong linkage between major emphasis upon new housing construction inserted at all income levels and dispersal of low- and moderate-income households outside the areas where they are now concentrated. All feasible options containing the former also involve the latter. All but two of the nine such options containing the latter involve the former.

- Dispersal is best accomplished through major multi-level insertion of new units because new units must be used to place low- and moderate-income households in new-growth areas. However, this can be done to some extent by marginally augmenting a basic "trickle-down" strategy with some new building of low- and moderate-income housing on dispersed sites as in Options 5-D and 6-D.

- However, the reason why major multi-level insertion of new units requires dispersal is not obvious. The main reason is that concentrating large-scale new construction of low- and moderate-income housing solely within inner-city decaying areas is not really feasible. Most moderate-income households do not want to live in such areas, and investors hesitate to risk even limited equity capital there because of adverse environmental conditions. Public housing can be concentrated there. But most governments at all levels have concluded that large-scale public housing projects in such areas simply aggravate the problems of concentrated poverty.

   a. At first glance, it might appear that large-scale multi-level insertion of new housing could be accommodated solely within inner-city decaying areas through All-Out Enrichment there. But experience shows that such major inner-city clearance and redevelopment would require relocation of many displaced low- and moderate-income households outside the areas where they are now concentrated. (Large-scale urban renewal had this effect in many cities; for example, St. Louis.) This requires a form of dispersal, even though it might mainly involve occupancy of existing older homes rather than new ones by the displaced households.

   b. This implies that All-Out Enrichment Only really contains an internal inconsistency; it is not a practically feasible option because of this displacement effect. Hence, Options 3-ABCDEFG are all nonfeasible. Nevertheless, we have left this Spatial Emphasis Option in our matrix because its nonfeasibility is not obvious, and some people are seriously proposing this as a desirable national strategy (especially those who decry the "crisis of our cities").

● Counteracting existing physical decay in inner-city areas probably also requires at least some dispersal. Former HUD Secretary Romney and others have recently made some strong statements about the grim future of many of our large cities if the nation does not take effective steps to halt—and counteract—such decay.

   a. Trying to counteract such decay without dispersal requires focusing remedial action upon pumping money into these areas through larger income maintenance and social service delivery. Then private markets would hopefully respond by improving the physical environment in response to the residents' expanded incomes.

   b. We are skeptical that much physical improvement would be forthcoming from such options. Private investors are not likely to sink risk capital into concentrated poverty areas without subsidies, especially since households who can afford non-directly subsidized new housing will not move there.

   c. Perhaps large-scale rehabilitation would occur through private action in response to higher incomes among households in these areas. This is the assumption that underlies Options 2-B and 2-C. However, experience with large-scale rehabilitation programs indicates that they also displace occupants of the units being upgraded—almost as completely as clearance and new construction. Hence, it is by no means certain that large-scale rehabilitation could occur in inner-city areas without at least some dispersal required by the relocation of displaced households.

    d. Thus, the feasible non-dispersal options that involve some anti-
       poverty efforts but only minimal direct emphasis upon physical rede-
       velopment of inner-city decaying areas (Options 2-BCD) are not
       likely to generate much physical redevelopment—even rehabilitation.
       And if they do, they will become transformed into some other type
       of option involving some dispersal.

- Dispersal of low- and moderate-income households outside of areas
  where they are now concentrated through deliberate use of direct housing subsidies is not a politically popular policy. In fact, President Nixon
  has specifically stated his opposition to it, unless the communities concerned accept such housing voluntarily (as very few have done). Yet
  this analysis indicates that such dispersal can be avoided only at the
  price of failing to counteract effectively the spreading physical decay in
  large parts of our biggest cities.

    a. The Grand Strategy Matrix thus illustrates the indissoluble linkage in
      the quality of life in most different portions of each metropolitan
      area. Those portions that have avoided the direct problems associated
      with poverty by deliberately excluding low- and moderate-income
      housing cannot continue to do so without condemning large parts
      of older central cities to continued—and worsening—physical decay.
      Thus, an important part of the responsibility for the future quality
      of life in inner-city areas rests squarely upon the decisions and actions
      of those living in more affluent portions of each metropolitan area.
      They cannot correctly argue that inner-city problems "are not their
      concern," because their refusal to stop excluding the relatively poor
      helps cause and sustain those problems.

    b. At the same time, it is important to remember that significant dis-
      persal does not require locating low- and moderate-income house-
      holds in every block throughout each metropolitan area, or even in
      every community. It only requires the entry of a large number of
      such households into portions of the metropolitan area where they
      are not now concentrated. However, such entry should be spread out
      among enough different places so that it does not lead to a renewed
      concentration of poverty in the newly-entered areas sometime in the
      near future.

- *The present combination of options that the federal government has
  apparently chosen is not really feasible in the long run.* We indicated
  earlier that we believe present policies amounted to (1) something
  between the "Contained Decay" and "Non-Capital Enrichment Only"
  Options, and (2) something between the "All-Out New Construction
  Plus Minimal Anti-Poverty" and "All-Out New Construction Plus Anti-
  Poverty" Options. However, the matrix indicates that all combinations
  of these four options are internally inconsistent for at least one reason
  or another. The major inconsistency is that the federal government

cannot long continue to subsidize major insertions of new housing at
low- and moderate-income levels without either causing major dispersal or engaging in major physical redevelopment of decaying inner-city
areas, as explained above.

   a. Up to now, we believe this inconsistency has been masked by the
spatial concentration of new moderate-income insertions in the
peripheral portions of central cities. These areas are neither inner-city
decaying neighborhoods nor suburbs. But they can absorb only a
limited amount of newly-built moderate-income housing.

   b. Shifting to much less emphasis upon new construction-oriented subsidies (as in "Accelerated 'Trickle-Down,' Marginally Augmented"
Options) would make feasible the avoidance of either major dispersal or major physical redevelopment of inner-city decaying areas, as
in Option 2-D.

4. Although our primary purpose in conducting this study was to provide
others with an objective view of federal housing subsidies for their own
decision-making, we were also asked to state our own policy preferences. We
believe the best feasible choice from the Grand Strategy Matrix at this time
is Option 6-F. It combines the "Non-Capital Enrichment Plus Dispersal Plus
Delayed Redevelopment" Option with the "Mixed Option" Strategy concerning levels of insertion of new units. We prefer this combination because:

- *It involves a significant degree of dispersal,* which we believe is essential
to both the long-range and short-range amelioration of the most pressing
inner-city problems in our society.

- *It initially emphasizes income maintenance and better social services
delivery, rather than physical redevelopment, for inner-city areas.* We
believe eventual physical redevelopment of these areas is appropriate,
but it cannot produce effective results until dispersal is underway, and
until the residents of these areas have higher incomes.

- *It makes use of a variety of housing subsidy approaches*—including direct and indirect, new construction-oriented and existing inventory-
oriented ones—rather than emphasizing any one type or approach exclusively. We believe this Mixed Options Strategy is appropriate to the complex housing needs of our society, and allows better adaptation of program instruments to local needs in each area.

- *It contains major emphasis upon direct income maintenance.* The biggest
single cause of housing problems in our society is poverty, and a crucial
ingredient in combatting poverty is giving more money to those who
cannot earn their way out of poverty independently.

- *It does not call for placing an unrealistically high priority on housing in
the allocation of national resources.* We believe that both "All-Out"
Options (7 and G) are unrealistic because they assume that Americans
want to make improvement of housing almost the top priority domestic

policy objective. We do not think this is the case—although housing has a surprisingly high priority already, judging from the size of federal subsidies it receives.

• Naturally, our preference represents only one opinion among many. We believe the real contribution of our analysis consists of our presenting a method of approaching this incredibly complex subject that will help others arrive at better informed and more effective policy preferences of their own.

Notes

1. Charles L. Schultze, Edward R. Fried, Alice M. Rivlin, and Nancy H. Teeters, *Setting National Priorities: The 1973 Budget* (Washington, D.C., 1972), p. 176.
2. John B. Lansing, Charles Wade Clifton, and James N. Morgan, *New Homes and Poor People* (Ann Arbor: Institute for Social Research of the University of Michigan, 1969).

7

The Overall Effectiveness of Current Housing Subsidies

Method of Evaluation

1. No simple and reliable overall evaluation of the "total effectiveness" of all existing federal housing subsidies is possible. There are too many different subsidies, serving too many varied objectives. Therefore, we will examine the effectiveness of all current subsidies together in meeting each of their *primary objectives*. We will then present a more general analysis of how well they are meeting their *secondary objectives*. (Both types of objectives were identified in Chapter 1, but are also set forth in chart 7-1 for convenient reference.) Comments concerning the effectiveness of subsidies in conforming to the *criteria of desirability* were presented in Chapter 4.

2. Crucial to such evaluation is the standard against which the performance of all housing subsidies together is compared. The most important possible standards are (1) their past performances, (2) the magnitude of the problem to which each objective is a response, and (3) official national housing goals. We will use all three standards where relevant.

3. We will first discuss the need to view the *housing-oriented performance* of federal housing subsidies in light of certain *non-housing functions* they have been required to perform.

How Nonhousing Functions Distort the Housing-Oriented Performance of Housing Subsidies

1. Federal housing subsidies ostensibly aimed at meeting housing needs are also compelled to bear large "excess burdens" of coping with major social problems other than providing shelter. This distorts the shelter-oriented effectiveness of such subsidies. That distortion must be taken into account when assessing overall effectiveness.

   - The most significant of these nonhousing problems are *urban poverty*, the *destructive behavior* of thousands of multi-problem households, and the terrible environments caused by the *large-scale poverty concentration* generated by the "trickle-down" process of urban development.
   - Society could best deal with these serious problems by such nonhousing

105

Chart 7–1

Specific Objectives of Federal Housing Subsidy Programs
(From Chapter 1)

Primary Objectives

- Providing housing assistance to low-income and moderate-income house-holds by enabling such households now living in substandard quality housing to occupy decent units, and by aiding such households who now pay inordinately high percentages of their incomes to live in decent units.
- Providing housing assistance to numerous specific groups in the same manner as described above. These groups include the elderly, Indians, per-sons displaced by government action, etc.
- Encouraging homeownership among households, regardless of their in-comes.
- Stimulating the economy by increasing activity in the housing industry.
- Increasing the total available supply of decent quality dwelling units.
- Improving the quality of deteriorated neighborhoods.

Secondary Objectives

- Providing housing assistance to colleges.
- Stabilizing the annual output of the housing industry at a high level.
- Encouraging housing innovations that improve design, reduce costs, and improve quality.
- Creating opportunities for employment, entrepreneurship, and training among residents of low-income areas.
- Encouraging maximum feasible participation of private enterprise and capital in meeting housing needs.
- Achieving greater spatial dispersion of low- and moderate-income housing outside areas of concentrated poverty.

programs as adequate income maintenance, creation of jobs, large-scale family and personal counseling, major reform of the criminal justice sys-tem, and dispersal of the poor throughout nonpoor areas. However, neither public opinion in general, nor Congress, nor the Administration appears willing to bear the costs of carrying out these other programs at the scale necessary to cope with the problems concerned.

- Consequently, some direct housing subsidy programs are used as indirect means of dealing with these problems, even though they are not well suited to that purpose. As a result, the effectiveness of these programs in providing shelter is seriously reduced.
- The public housing program has been especially injured by such "excess burdens" because it is used to cope with all three problems. The public housing operating-cost subsidy is a disguised income supplement for the very poor; many public housing projects have become "storage bins" for multi-problem families rejected by all other areas; and the concentra-

tion of such families within large public housing projects makes those projects nonviable environments. The resulting "failure" of public housing to provide "a decent home" is not really due to the nature of this subsidy program at all. Rather, it is caused by administration of the program so as to make up partly for inadequacies in more direct remedies to these other problems.

2. Consequently, much of the recent outcry about the "failure" of direct housing subsidy programs has arisen through the critics' failure to distinguish between difficulties generated by using those programs to cope with non-housing problems, and difficulties generated by the inherent nature of housing subsidies themselves.

    *   For example, total capital invested in subsidized housing (exclusive of tax shelters) that must deal with these problems will inescapably have a lower rate of return, and much greater percentage of defaults, than total capital invested in meeting "normal" housing needs.
    *   Therefore, in evaluating program effectiveness, it is wrong to use the same standards concerning per-unit costs, rates of return, and default percentages for both subsidized and nonsubsidized housing. Direct housing subsidy programs that appear disastrously ineffective or costly by "normal" evaluation standards may nevertheless be desirable because of their even partial success in coping with nonshelter problems.

3. Until society is willing to carry out other programs that directly address these major nonshelter problems on a much more adequate scale, it may be more effective to use direct housing subsidy programs to help cope with them than to do little or nothing about them—even though this causes the housing subsidy programs to appear ineffective or very costly in providing shelter per se.

    *   To reduce or eliminate direct housing subsidy programs now being used for these nonshelter purposes without simultaneously expanding other programs aimed directly at those purposes would be a hollow victory for the poor households now benefiting from direct housing subsidies.
    *   On the other hand, if alternative programs for dealing with these non-shelter problems were adopted, the use of direct housing subsidy programs could be significantly altered or even reduced.

How Effectively Are Housing Subsidies Currently Providing Housing Assistance to Low- and Moderate-Income Households Who Need Such Assistance?

1. The effectiveness of current housing subsidy programs in meeting the *physical* housing needs of these households is quite different from their effectiveness in meeting the *financial* housing needs of such households.

- In 1966, according to an Office of Economic Opportunity survey, 5.0 million substandard quality housing units were occupied by low- and moderate-income households, including single-person households under sixty-five years old (or 3.9 million excluding the latter). About 2.2 million such units (44 percent) were in rural areas; the other 2.8 million were in urban areas. Current federal housing subsidy programs can be regarded as effective in meeting *physical* housing needs to the extent that they provide replacements for these substandard units, and make them available to low- and moderate-income households.

- In 1969, according to an Urban Institute estimate, about 16.6 million households—or 10.9 million excluding single-person households—would have had to spend over 25 percent of their incomes to pay for decent quality housing at the average prevailing price. All of these households had low or moderate incomes. Current federal housing subsidy programs can be regarded as effective in meeting the *financial* housing needs of these households to the extent that they provide additional purchasing power (presumably oriented towards housing) for such households without generating excessive housing price increases.

- These data indicate that there were about twice as many low- and moderate-income households with financial housing needs as with physical housing needs in 1969.

2. Current direct housing subsidy programs are designed primarily to meet the physical housing needs of low- and moderate-income households. They do so by creating new or rehabilitated housing units for their occupancy. Only rent supplements, the public housing leasing program, and public housing operating-cost subsidies aim at meeting the *financial* housing needs of these households. Even they are often tied to the creation of new or rehabilitated units.

3. From 1967 through 1971, direct federal housing subsidies generated about 1.3 million additional housing units for low- and moderate-income households. Assuming that 95 percent of these units were in urban areas, direct housing subsidies thus generated enough units in these five years to replace 48 percent of all urban substandard units occupied by low- and moderate-income households as of 1966 (or 63 percent of such units excluding those occupied by single-person households under sixty-five).

   - If production of directly subsidized units continues at a level of 400,000 per year (as exceeded in 1970 and 1971), and 95 percent are urban, then by the end of 1976, enough subsidized units will have been produced to replace all of the substandard urban units occupied by low- and moderate-income households as of 1966.

     a. This calculation assumes that any more units so occupied that have become substandard since 1966 are offset by nonsubsidized upgrading of other substandard units.

b. It.is not likely that every particular low- and moderate-income household that lived in a substandard unit in 1966 will actually have
moved into a new subsidized unit by 1976. However, the new subsidized units will certainly have had an immensely favorable impact
upon the physical housing choices of these households.

4.   Under the same assumptions as above, by the end of 1976, only 167,000
directly subsidized new units will have been created for low- and moderate-
income households in *rural* areas. However, 2.2 million such households in
rural areas occupied substandard units in 1966. Even if ten percent of all
directly subsidized units are rural, rather than the five percent assumed
above, the number of such units created in rural areas in the 1966–1976
decade will equal only 15 percent of the rural physical housing needs of
this group as of 1966.

5.   Although about two-thirds of all the directly subsidized units mentioned
above were for moderate-income households, that share has been rising
lately and probably exceeds 75 percent at present. Yet no reliable conclusions can be drawn about whether current subsidy programs are more effective at serving moderate-income households than low-income households in
relation to the needs of both groups.

• We do not know exactly how the total physical or financial housing
needs of both groups *combined* break down *separately*.

• Moreover, "chain effects" of moves induced by new moderate-income
housing can help meet the housing needs of low-income households too.

6.   The above considerations lead to the following conclusions about the overall effectiveness of current housing subsidies in serving this primary objective:

• They are *very effective* in meeting the *physical* housing needs of *urban*
low- and moderate-income households combined.

• They are *quite ineffective* in meeting the *physical* housing needs of *rural*
low- and moderate-income households combined, or either type separately.

It should be emphasized that there are far more urban than rural low-
and moderate-income households, even though substandard housing
was relatively evenly divided between urban and rural areas in 1966.
In that year, urban households in this income group outnumbered
rural ones 29.1 million to 4.3 million (excluding single-person households under age sixty-five). Hence, current direct subsidy programs are
effectively meeting the physical housing needs of the vast majority of
low- and moderate-income households.

• They are *only partly effective* in meeting the *financial* housing needs
of either group—but they were not really designed to do so.

7.   In relation to official national housing goals, current direct housing subsidy
programs are still producing added units at well below an average of

600,000 additional units per year from 1968 to 1978. Annual production of such units was rapidly accelerating towards that level from 1967 through 1970, but has leveled off in 1971 and 1972 still well below that target. It appears unlikely that production of directly subsidized units will rise far enough above the 600,000 average for the remainder of the decade to achieve that average by 1978. However, such production could be pushed closer to the target level by continued high level appropriations for subsidy funds from Congress.

✔ **How Effectively Are Housing Subsidies Currently Providing Housing Assistance to Other Special Groups in the Population They Are Designed to Serve?**

It has proved impractical to obtain detailed enough information about what group members are occupying directly subsidized units to answer this question.

How Effectively Are Housing Subsidies Encouraging Homeownership?

1. In 1970, 62.9 percent of all occupied housing units in the United States were owner-occupied. This fraction increased only slightly from 1960, when it was 61.9 percent. Nevertheless, it exceeds the percentage of owner-occupied units in most Western European nations significantly—particularly that in their urban areas. This is shown in table 7-1.

2. The biggest subsidy incentive encouraging homeownership is the deductibility of mortgage interest and property taxes from federally taxable

Table 7-1

Percentage of Owner-Occupied Housing in Five Western European Nations, 1966

Nation	Total	Urban	Rural
West Germany	35.3%	16.4%	47.8%
Sweden	36.0%	20.0%	65.0%
Netherlands	29.3%	17.2%	48.7%
France	46.5%	33.0%	57.5%
United Kingdom	43.9%	43.6%	45.1%

Source: Howard R. Moskof, "Foreign Housing Subsidy Systems: Alternative Approaches." Paper submitted to the Subcommittee on Housing Panels, House Committee on Banking and Currency, 92nd Congress.

Table 7-2

Number of Subsidized Units Produced by Type, 1968-1971

Type of Tenure	New Construction	Existing Units	Total
Rental	762,370	52,960	815,330
Ownership	462,400	83,000	545,400
Total	1,224,770	135,960	1,360,730
Percentage Ownership	37.8%	61.0%	40.1%

Note: The figures for "Existing Units" cover rehabilitation; they do *not* include good quality existing units sold under subsidized programs.

Source: U.S. Department of Housing and Urban Development.

income. Although there is no way of calculating precisely what effects this huge subsidy has had, they are undoubtedly significant.

3. Current direct housing subsidy programs have created somewhat more rental housing than ownership housing, as shown in table 7-2.

    About 40 percent of the new units added under subsidized programs have been ownership units. When use of existing units for Section 235 and FHA programs is also considered, the proportion of ownership units rises to about 45 percent. Considering the incomes of the groups served, and the fact that low- and moderate-income households are predominantly renters, these programs can still be considered favorable to promotion of homeownership.

How Effectively Are Housing Subsidies Stimulating the Economy by Increasing Activity in the Housing Industry?

1. Direct housing subsidies have played a key role in stimulating the housing industry since 1968. They have accounted for a rapidly rising share of total starts, as indicated above. In fact, average annual production of conventional non-directly subsidized housing has not changed much since 1955. It was actually lower during 1970 and 1971 than in the early 1960s and late 1950s, as shown in table 7-3. The relative share of unsubsidized conventional housing units in total production has declined since 1955. In addition to the rise in the proportion of directly subsidized units, mobile home shipments have increased steadily. They rose from an average of seven percent of total new dwelling units in the late 1950s, to about 20 percent in 1970 and 1971.

2. Since direct housing subsidies became an absolutely and relatively significant factor in housing production (after 1966), average annual total housing output has increased 26 percent, as compared to its level from 1956 through

Table 7–3

Conventional Housing Starts as a Proportion of Total
New Starts, 1955–1971

Time Period	Annual Average Number of Conventional Housing Starts, Not Directly Subsidized	As a Percentage of Average Total Starts, Including Directly Subsidized Units
1955–1959	1,387,192	97.4%
1960–1964	1,422,505	97.0%
1965–1969	1,297,156	92.0%
1970–1971	1,343,395	75.7%

Source: Table 2–4.

1966. (As considered here, total housing output includes mobile homes.) Direct subsidies have certainly not accounted for all of this big increase. Nevertheless, in 1970 and 1971, they generated one out of every five total housing starts. Moreover, indirect subsidies have undoubtedly attracted more total investment into owner-occupied homes than would otherwise have gone into housing. Hence, housing subsidies have definitely increased activity in the housing industry.

3. Because of the stimulus of direct housing subsidies, plus unusually favorable mortgage finance conditions, total housing production in 1971 for the first time equalled the planned average of 2.6 million additional units called for by the official national housing goals. A total of 2,581,070 new units were produced, and enough existing ones rehabilitated to pass the 2.6 million mark. Moreover, through the first five months of 1972, housing production was about 20 percent ahead of the all-time record 1971 level. Hence, direct housing subsidies are contributing to attainment of official housing production goals, at least for the time being. They are certainly not the only factor causing this outcome, however.

How Effectively Are Housing Subsidies Increasing the Total Available Supply of Decent Dwelling Units?

1. Additions to the supply of decent dwelling units are the net result of new housing construction, plus rehabilitation of substandard units, minus demolitions and other removals of decent units from the inventory. Net removals averaged 630,000 units per year in the 1960s, and are probably now averaging about 700,000 units per year. However, some of the units removed each year are substandard. Thus, the average annual creation of 2.2 million new

units in 1970 and 1971 actually resulted in an annual average net addition to the supply of decent dwelling units of about 1.7 million units (if 200,000 of the units removed each year were substandard).

2. In these two years, an average of 432,000 new directly subsidized units were built. Hence, direct housing subsidies accounted for about one-fourth of the net additions to the supply of decent dwelling units during the past two years. As noted earlier, this performance is vastly superior to that typical before 1968, but lower than that called for by the official national housing goals.

How Effectively Are Housing Subsidies Improving the Quality of Deteriorated Neighborhoods?

1. Available data are not adequate to provide a reliable answer to this question. However, our field work and analysis have led to the following tentative conclusions relevant to it:

    - Creation of large-scale new subsidized housing projects in deteriorated neighborhoods definitely upgrades the environment there. We found several examples of such projects in the cities we visited.

    - Directly subsidized housing units comprise virtually the only new housing being built in the most deteriorated portions of large cities. Unsubsidized private capital is simply not being invested in these areas, which private lenders regard as involving excessive risks. Hence, insofar as any housing is improving the quality of these areas, it is directly subsidized housing.

    - Most directly subsidized housing in metropolitan areas is being placed within central cities. We were unable to obtain nationwide data concerning the location of such housing from HUD. However, in those metropolitan areas where we procured accurate information, the vast majority of new subsidized units were being located in central cities—though not mainly in deteriorated neighborhoods.

    - In some inner-city areas, poorly administered FHA lending under high risk programs was contributing to faster neighborhood turnover and deterioration than would otherwise have occurred. The causes of such poor administration were discussed in chapter 5.

        a. Such lending practices were concentrated in a relatively small number of cities, and mainly involved market rate mortgages with low down payments or liberal credit terms, rather than subsidized mortgages.

        b. In the affected areas, unusually high percentages of defaults concentrated in a few neighborhoods produced faster than usual withdrawal of middle-class households, and higher than usual abandonment rates. However, these conditions were caused by major housing subsidy programs (in contrast to the Section 223 and 237 programs) in only a very few neighborhoods—many fewer than were positively affected by subsidized units in major programs.

2. We believe effective improvement of many badly deteriorated inner-city neighborhoods will require some new legal mechanisms for "neighborhood management," plus major subsidies for improving community conditions. Housing subsidies alone cannot effectively cope with the adverse conditions in such neighborhoods.

- Better "neighborhood management" is required because the adverse "spillover effects" from a few badly maintained units can drastically reduce the quality of life in the entire area, and cause spreading blight. Yet no single private or public agent now has either the power or the resources to act swiftly enough to counteract such poor maintenance soon after it appears.
  a. It would be desirable for HUD to finance experiments with new legal forms of local property management intervention in designated older neighborhoods, using both private and public agents as "intervenors" or "managers."
  b. Moreover, revised foreclosure rules are necessary in almost all inner-city areas to enable much faster public intervention when building abandonment occurs.
- Ultimately, conditions in the worst inner-city areas cannot be improved in the long run without some dispersal aimed at reducing concentrated poverty, in our opinion. This was discussed in chapter 6.
- Since almost all current housing subsidies concentrate on improving individual *dwelling units* (or groups of them), they are not adequate instruments for coping with adverse *community conditions* existing outside individual dwelling units, or arising from interactions among such units. Thus, current housing subsidies alone cannot achieve the "suitable living environment" aspect of the nation's basic housing goal.

How Effectively Are Housing Subsidies Achieving Their Secondary Objectives?

1. We were unable to determine how effectively such subsidies were providing housing assistance to colleges because of the difficulty of determining how large the needs for such assistance were nationwide.

2. Direct housing subsidies have not been very effective in stablizing the output of the housing industry at a high level. This is shown by the following evidence:

- The industry's output has been less stable since direct subsidies became significant (after 1966) than before. During the period from 1956 through 1966, annual total housing production averaged 1.548 million units. The highest output year was 16 percent above this average, and the lowest 14 percent below it. The average annual *absolute change in total output* equalled ten percent of average total output. From 1967 through 1971, total production averaged 1.957 million units per year. The highest year was 32 percent above this, and the lowest 20 percent below it. The average annual absolute change in total output equalled 13 percent of average total output.

- There has been no consistent relationship between changes in the level of directly subsidized production and changes in total production. For example, since 1966, the biggest annual change in level of subsidies was a rise of 234,000 from 1969 to 1970. This was a stabilizing force, since nonsubsidized production dropped 267,000 in the same period. But the second biggest change in subsidized output—a rise of 72,000 from 1967 to 1968—was destabilizing, because nonsubsidized production rose 152,000 in the same period.

3. It is our impression that housing subsidies in general have not encouraged design and other innovations very effectively. However, the specific subsidies used in Operation Breakthrough did have significant innovating impacts. They interested many large industrial firms in housing, and obtained major institutional changes in building codes and union practices in many states.

4. We were unable to obtain sufficient data to assess the effectiveness of housing subsidies at creating opportunities for employment, entrepreneurship, and training among residents of low-income areas.

5. Direct housing subsidies appear to have been very effective in encouraging maximum feasible participation of private enterprise and capital in meeting housing needs. The interest subsidy programs (Section 235 and Section 236) in particular have attracted a great deal of private investment capital into creating housing for households who would otherwise not be furnished with new units by private markets, and might not be furnished with any decent quality units (although the latter conclusion is far less certain than the former).

- The Section 236 program provides attractive tax shelter features for high tax bracket private investors. Consequently, thousands of investors have put capital into this program who would never have done so without this advantage, insofar as we could determine. Syndication of Section 236 projects by stock brokerage firms and investment bankers has diverted many millions of dollars into this program that would otherwise probably have been invested in common stocks.

- However, the coincidence of large congressional funding for direct housing subsidies with enormous in-flows of private savings into mortgage-oriented institutions has greatly facilitated achievement of this goal during 1970, 1971, and 1972.

6. Direct housing subsidies appear to have been administered in a way that has made them relatively ineffective at achieving greater dispersal of low- and moderate-income households throughout metropolitan areas. This failing has not resulted from the inherent nature of such subsidies. Rather, it stems from the unwillingness of federal officials to try generating such dispersal through overall planning of where subsidized units should be located in each metropolitan area. Consequently, most of the subsidized units inside metropolitan areas have been located in central cities not far from existing poverty concentrations, insofar as we can tell from limited available data. This objective may be better served in the future by application of HUD's new site selection criteria. However, it is too early to determine the impact of those criteria.

8 Recommendations for Action

This final chapter brings together the specific recommendations developed throughout the book. Data and analyses supporting these conclusions are not presented here since they are included in earlier chapters. Our recommendations have been grouped in a manner somewhat different from the organization of the earlier chapters. We have tried to eliminate *conclusions* here and focus solely upon *recommendations for action*. However, it was necessary to include a few conclusions for clarity, so there is some repetition from earlier portions of the report.

Recommendations Concerning the Basic Role of Housing Subsidies

For a relatively small, but absolutely large, group of Americans, inadequate housing is a critical deficiency. It is part of a cluster of deficiencies in their lives associated mainly with poverty.

1. Our society could best deal with serious poverty problems by such nonhousing programs as adequate income maintenance, creation of jobs, large-scale family and personal counseling, major reform of the criminal justice system, and dispersal of the poor throughout nonpoor areas. We strongly urge that these programs be given high-priority consideration as key steps in attacking what is often called the nation's "housing problem." However, at present, neither public opinion in general, nor Congress, nor the Administration appears willing to bear the costs of carrying out these other programs at the scale necessary to cope with the problems concerned.

2. Until we are willing to carry out other programs that directly address these major nonshelter problems on a much more adequate scale, it will be more effective to use direct housing subsidy programs to help cope with them than to do little or nothing about them—even though this causes housing subsidy programs to appear ineffective or very costly in providing shelter per se.

3. Even if adequate nonhousing programs related to poverty were adopted, we would still need large-scale direct housing subsidies for new construction to expand the supply of decent housing units available to low- and moderate-income households. Otherwise, rising housing prices and costs would partly offset any higher incomes (or housing allowances) received by the poor.

117

Recommendations Concerning Housing
Subsidies in Deteriorating Areas

Other than poverty in general, the most serious housing-related problems are those connected with deteriorating neighborhood environments in older urban areas. To respond adequately to problems of neighborhood decay, public policy must include far more comprehensive actions than subsidies aimed at improving physical dwelling units. Yet significant amounts of direct housing subsidies will also be required.

1. Some new mechanism for *neighborhood management* is needed to provide for a more orderly quality of life in inner-city decaying areas—whatever future strategy is adopted toward them. These areas contain fragmented property ownership, plus very low incomes, plus very low levels of personal and physical security. As a result, social and personal pathologies spill over from one household or housing unit to others nearby. Few local resources are available to respond with either stronger social controls or compensating investments.

   - The most crucial single improvement in urban affairs would be effective local surveillance or other arrangements providing high level personal and property security in these decaying urban neighborhoods. This in turn requires radical reform in the existing system of criminal justice, which simply does not work in such areas.
   - It would be desirable for HUD to finance experiments with new legal forms of local property management intervention in designated older neighborhoods, using both private and public agents as "intervenors" or "managers."
   - Moreover, revised foreclosure rules are necessary in almost all inner-city areas to enable much faster public intervention when building abandonment occurs.

2. Continued concentration of poverty in older central-city neighborhoods will undermine the effectiveness of most physical improvements made there. Hence, some type of purely voluntary dispersal is essential to any long-range upgrading of the quality of life in these areas.

   - Dispersal into new-growth suburban areas requires subsidies that allow low- and moderate-income occupancy of brand new units. Therefore, the greater the social policy emphasis on dispersal as part of any strategy, the more important the role of new construction-oriented housing subsidies.
   - Housing subsidies alone will probably not cause much direct outward movement from inner-city poverty areas into dispersed locations without specific incentives tied to such movement. Hence, HUD should require that a certain fraction of the initial occupants of all directly subsidized suburban housing—such as Section 236 and Section 235

units—consist of households moving directly from inner-city areas. We suggest that 20 to 25 percent require such eligibility.

3. HUD and FHA administrative practices concerning inner-city areas should be improved. Specifically:

- Greater understanding of the household and real estate economics of central-city neighborhoods is needed. Personnel handling subsidies in these areas should receive special training.
- Congress and the Office of Management and Budget should change existing personnel restrictions so that HUD can expand its staff. Otherwise, it cannot possibly deal effectively with its immensely expanded workload, and further scandals will result.
- HUD should adopt explicit policies adapted to inner-city areas, and those policies should be clearly explained to local FHA administrators and staff members. Actions carried out in fulfillment of these policies should be monitored.
- Workloads of FHA personnel should be adjusted to allow longer processing time for loans in more complicated areas.

4. FHA should not be made a semi-private separate agency outside HUD responsible only for nonsubsidized mortgage operations. FHA's nonsubsidized operations are profitable, and those profits should be used to help finance activities that aid the most needy households.

Recommendations Concerning the Costs of Meeting National Housing Needs

There is no way to fully meet either America's financial housing needs or its physical housing needs without incurring high annual budgetary costs. Whether it is worthwhile to incur high public costs in order to meet either type of housing need is a value judgment that must be decided politically and ethically. It cannot be decided scientifically.

Specific recommendations relating to *calculation* and *consideration* of housing needs and housing subsidy costs are as follows:

1. Future costs of housing subsidy programs and all other programs should be discounted before being compared with present dollars or with other future costs. This is consistent both with prevailing investment practices in the private sector and with congressional tendencies to weight near-future benefits more heavily than distant-future costs.
2. Costs that do not appear in the federal budget directly—but still must be paid by taxpayers—should certainly be included in calculating total subsidy costs.
   - It is extremely misleading to ignore nonbudgetary subsidy costs, espe-

cially since they form nearly two-thirds of all housing subsidy costs.

- Both annual and "lifetime" costs should be considered in making housing subsidy decisions. However, it is very difficult to forecast "lifetime" costs of many current federal housing subsidies, and a proposed housing allowance, because of uncertainties inherent in their design.

- It is unrealistic to regard contractual commitments for future spending as more binding than noncontractual commitments that, once made, would be extremely difficult to eliminate for political reasons. For example, once a nationwide housing allowance program was adopted, it would be very difficult to halt it politically—even though no contractual commitments beyond one year would be involved. Hence, it is just as important to examine future costs of such a program over a long period as it is to examine those contractually required by mortgage loans.

Recommendations Concerning the Proper Mix of Types of Housing Subsidies

An "optimal" set of housing subsidies should include several different types, rather than just one. We have arrived at the following specific recommendations concerning the most appropriate mix:

1. The housing program mix should contain both new construction-oriented subsidies and subsidies oriented toward more intensive use of the existing inventory. *Agree*

    - New construction-oriented subsidies have begun to produce significant effects because of their high levels of funding and output since 1968. We recommend continuation of direct new construction-oriented subsidies at about the level of 400,000 additional units per year for at least several more years.

    - Up to now, emphasis has been much stronger on new construction-oriented subsidies than on those that use the existing inventory. Therefore, it would be desirable to expand the latter type in the future to achieve a better overall balance.

    a. Present subsidies that effectively use existing housing units should be given relatively high priority for expansion—especially the public housing leasing program.

    b. Experiments testing a housing allowance program that are presently underway should be continued and given high-priority attention. However, no full-scale housing allowance program should be undertaken until more is known about its likely effects, if then.

    c. We do not now believe that a nationwide housing allowance program providing assistance to all households eligible on the basis of low income alone would be desirable. It seems too likely to cause undue

increases in housing rents and prices in many low-income neighborhoods.

   d. Experiments should also be conducted to test a new program allow-
      ing low- and moderate-income households to rent single-family homes
      repossessed by FHA. The rent supplement and public housing leas-
      ing programs could be modified to allow this.

 2. Local housing market conditions should have an important influence upon
   the mix of housing subsidy forms used in each area. New construction-
   oriented subsidies should be emphasized in areas with low vacancy rates in
   low-income housing or in general. Subsidies encouraging greater use of the
   existing inventory should be emphasized where vacancy rates are relatively
   high among decent quality units.

Recommendations Concerning the Nation's
Overall Housing Strategy

In our opinion, the type of national housing strategy best designed to serve the
long-run interests of the country as a whole would exhibit the following specific
characteristics:

1. *A significant degree of dispersal of low- and moderate-income households*
   into suburban areas and other neighborhoods where they do not now reside.
   We believe this is essential to both long-range and short-range improvement
   of the most pressing inner-city problems.
   - Consideration should be given to funding community impact grants
     made by HUD to communities that initially accept additional low- and
     moderate-income housing. Such grants would be "bonuses" designed to
     more than offset the added local public costs of new low- and moderate-
     income residents, at least for the first few years after their housing was
     established.
   - A variety of other dispersal-furthering tactics should also be considered,
     though their enumeration is beyond the scope of this study.
2. *Initial emphasis upon improved income maintenance and better social services delivery for inner-city areas*, rather than large-scale physical redevelopment there. We believe large-scale physical redevelopment of these areas
   will eventually be appropriate. But it probably cannot produce effective
   results until dispersal is underway, or at least until the residents of these
   areas have higher incomes.
3. *Use of a variety of housing subsidy approaches rather than exclusive emphasis upon any one approach.* We believe direct, indirect, new construction-
   oriented, existing inventory-oriented, supply-expanding, and demand-
   expanding subsidies all have significant roles in the most effective mix of
   subsidies. Hence, the "Mixed Options" strategy is the most appropriate to

the complex housing needs of our society. It also allows better adaptation of program instruments to local needs in each area.

4. *Major nationwide emphasis upon direct income maintenance and creation of jobs for the unemployed.* The biggest single cause of housing problems in our society is poverty. Crucial weapons in combating poverty are giving more money to those who cannot earn their way out of poverty independently, and creating jobs for those who could but are not now doing so.

5. *Placement of realistic priority on housing in the allocation of national resources and public funds.* In our opinion, since most Americans are relatively well housed, they do not believe improvement of housing should be the top priority domestic policy objective—although housing has a surprisingly high priority already, judging from the size of all types of federal subsidies it now receives. Hence, the national housing strategy should not be based upon the unrealistic assumption that enormous increases in resources—either public or private—will become available to cope with housing problems in the near future.

Recommendations Concerning Specific Existing Programs

1. *Administrative Improvements for All Existing Programs*
   - Much more effective income certification and recertification procedures need to be developed for all HUD housing programs. Although we encountered no concrete evidence on this subject, it was our strong impression from talking to both developers and HUD officials that many present occupants of subsidized housing units are falsifying their incomes. If this practice becomes widespread, it will subvert the effectiveness of HUD's programs and contribute to already prevalent cynicism towards the fairness of government action in general.
   - Long-term financing through direct loans from the federal government, or federally-guaranteed bonds issued by the Federal National Mortgage Association (FNMA), should be substituted for present "normal" FNMA financing of Section 235 and Section 236 loans. FNMA's nonguaranteed bonds require higher interest rates than would government-guaranteed bonds, or direct government loans. The difference in interest rates may be as large as two percent—which adds tremendously to the lifetime subsidy costs of Section 235 and Section 236 units.

     Although direct government loans would appear in the federal budget, federally-guaranteed FNMA bonds would not. If those bonds were used *only* to finance subsidized housing rather than nonsubsidized mortgages bought by FNMA, the resulting lower interest rates would not unduly benefit nonsubsidized borrowers.

- Households occupying units in *all* federally financed housing subsidy programs should receive far more extensive counseling than at present. Added funding for such counseling should be written into each program, and allowed as a standard part of project costs.

2. *Improvements in the Section 235 Program*
   - Very low-income households should not be encouraged to undertake homeownership because of the relative hardships imposed upon them in meeting unexpected operating costs, and the resulting high probability of default. Hence, more formal minimum income requirements should be instituted for Section 235 units.
   - Consideration should be given to creating a special mortgage payment insurance program to help moderate-income households meet their mortgage payments and avoid defaults even when they encountered unusual personal expenses or fluctuations in income.
   - Handling fees for recertification should be reduced, or eliminated altogether.
   - A stronger construction warranty from builders would be desirable.
   - More newly-built units should be located in low-income neighborhoods —especially in areas where there is a history of successful homeownership.
   - Administrative procedures concerning application of Section 235 financing to *existing* housing units should be tightened up and fully carried out so as to prevent overly high appraisals and approval of units in poor condition.

3. *Improvements in the Section 236 Program*
   - HUD should review estimated project costs with far more care and more emphasis upon actual local experience with existing Section 236 projects. This is necessary to avoid cost underestimation—especially of property taxes— and to prevent requests for rent increases arising very soon after a project is occupied.
   - The impact of previously approved Section 236 projects upon local market conditions should be thoroughly evaluated before additional developments are funded under this program.
   - The rate of return on low risk Section 236 projects should be reduced *relative* to that on high risk Section 236 projects as an inducement to investors to place more funds in the latter. High risk projects include those located in deteriorated areas and those with a high percentage of low-income occupants. The rates of return to investors can be altered by changing the Building and Sponsors Profit Allowance or other terms so as to create the differential mentioned above.
   - Nonprofit sponsors should be required to maintain an equity reserve, at least until full occupancy is achieved and preferably longer.
   - HUD should renegotiate commitments when local market conditions change markedly before construction begins.

- Site characteristics should be more carefully reviewed to avoid placement of 236 units on marginal land.
- Management capability should be evaluated more carefully when funds are initially allocated.
- To encourage long-term management interest, HUD should place heavy emphasis on the past experience of sponsors in making allocations for new developments.
- To improve incentives for good management, initial sponsors might be required to retain a permanent interest of 20 to 25 percent instead of being allowed to sell out fully to investors.
- Income limits should be related to the local median family income and should not be tied to public housing limits.
- In very low-income areas, rent supplements should be authorized for close to 100 percent of the units in a Section 236 project, rather than just 20 percent. This would encourage project development in the neediest neighborhoods where most moderate-income households refuse to live—and hence non-rent supplement units are hard to market.
- Minimum income limits should be established so that occupants will not be spending high fractions of their incomes for housing.
- More amenities should be allowed (e.g., air conditioning, carpets, swiming pools) so that 236 units will remain competitive with nonsubsidized units and hold middle-income occupants.
- More social services like security forces and tenant counseling should be available where needed, and included as allowable project costs.
- Community public relations programs should be mandatory, especially where rent supplement units are included, so as to minimize friction with surrounding property owners.

4. *Improvement in Public Housing Programs*
- A more adequate per-unit subsidy in lieu of taxes should be paid to the local governments that serve public housing units. It should be an amount close to what such units would pay if market rents were charged and assessments were made under normal local practices. This subsidy should be financed entirely by the federal government as part of its annual contribution, over and above debt service payments.
- Efficiency would be improved if one local housing authority covered each metropolitan area, and perhaps one statewide authority covered all communities outside of metropolitan areas. Legislation encouraging consolidation of smaller authorities by providing strong operating cost benefits from doing so might reduce the presently excessive number of local housing authorities.
- Most additional conventional and turnkey public housing units should be created in small-scale projects at scattered locations.
- All central-city public housing authorities should be allowed to operate

all their programs (including leasing) on a metropolitan areawide scale, without restriction to communities having local housing authorities or to the boundaries of the central city.

- No households should be ejected from public housing projects because of incomes above stated limits if they are willing to remain and pay specified minimum rents. This would assist in covering operating costs in many projects.

- Relative emphasis should shift from conventional and turnkey public housing programs to public housing leasing. This would aid in scatteration of households throughout each metropolitan area, and could make more intensive use of the existing inventory where warranted.

- Whether or not public housing programs should be expanded within large cities depends upon society's policy choices concerning nonhousing objectives, rather than the effectiveness of these programs as housing instruments per se.

- The public housing operating cost subsidy (created under the so-called "Brooke Amendment") should be abolished as soon as it can be replaced by more adequate income maintenance. That aid should be paid to public housing occupants by some agency other than HUD, or at least administered by some agency other than the local housing authority.

5. *Improvements in the Rent Supplement Program*
    - Rent supplement financing should be applicable to existing standard quality housing units, not just to new or rehabilitated units.
    - Households who receive the subsidy in a given unit, and then earn higher incomes and become ineligible, should be eligible again if their incomes fall back into the permissible range. At present, they have to move out.
    - The workable program requirement, and all other requirements for specific community approval, should be abolished.

Recommendations Concerning the Degree of Centralization in Administration of Housing Subsidies

Under present conditions, we believe the basic initiative for development of subsidized housing in each metropolitan area should remain with individual builders, developers, sponsors, and housing authorities. Such decentralized administration is likely to be more effective than reliance upon a single areawide allocation agency, for reasons described in chapter 6. However, we recommend the following actions concerning this general subject:

1. HUD should seek to impose some overall rationality on this decentralized allocation process by using standardized locational criteria in evaluating each proposed project. Such criteria have already been developed, although they

will have to be modified in practice as experience with them accumulates.

2. The effectiveness of the current system would be improved if individual communities were unable to exclude subsidized housing through manipulation of building codes and zoning ordinances. HUD should therefore press for statewide codes and reasonable nonexclusionary zoning.

3. Enough uncertainty exists about the effectiveness of a single areawide housing allocation agency to warrant several experiments involving such agencies. We recommend immediate initiation of such experiments in five to ten metropolitan areas with varying characteristics. One agency in each area should be created or designated and given authority over allocation of all HUD funds for subsidized housing in its area.

Appendix
Abbreviated Summary of Major Existing Federal Housing Subsidies, in Terms of "Pure" Housing Subsidy Forms and Other Major Characteristics

Section 235

1. Home ownership subsidy for moderate-income households using newly constructed, rehabilitated, or existing single-family units (including those in cooperatives).
2. Combines an interest rate reduction subsidy, an extended loan term, increased loan coverage and interest deductibility subsidy for homeowner-occupants.
3. Also has some features of a housing allowance, since amount of interest reduction subsidy varies, depending upon occupant's income. That subsidy equals amount required to reduce debt cost to at least 20 percent of occupant's income—with ceiling set by difference between market rate of interest and one percent.

Section 236

1. Rental housing subsidy for moderate-income households, using newly constructed or rehabilitated multi-family units.
2. Subsidy structure very similar to Section 235 in principles and form, but for rental units. Combines an interest rate reduction subsidy, increased loan coverage (up to 100 percent for nonprofit sponsors), and accelerated depreciation for investors.
3. Has same variable interest rate subsidy as Section 235, but reduces total rent to at least 25 percent of occupant's income with same type of ceiling.
4. Rent supplement subsidy (described below) can be combined with Section 236 program to make units in these buildings available to low-income households.

Low-Rent Public Housing

Rental housing subsidy program for low-income households (those with incomes generally below $4,400 per year), with four major variations as follows:

1. *Conventional Public Housing*
   - Local housing authority floats bonds to pay for construction of multi-family units, and federal government pays debt service on bonds (both interest and principal) annually.

- Until recently, local housing authority paid all operating costs out of rents charged occupants.
- Since local housing authority pays local government only 10 percent of rents in lieu of property taxes, this program also involves property tax abatement subsidy by local government.

2. *Turnkey Public Housing*
- Private builder finds site and builds units for local housing authority after it approves plans. Then local authority buys units from builder and uses them for low-rent housing as in conventional program.
- Financing and local tax subsidies same as conventional program, but initiative and administration during construction handled by builders, not by housing authorities. Results in faster construction.
- One variation (Turnkey III) can be used to build single-family homes purchased by low-income households with public housing subsidy.

3. *Public Housing Leasing* (*Section 23*)
- Local housing authority leases existing rental units from owners (or new ones built for this purpose) at market rental rates and then subleases to low-income households at lower rents—absorbing difference as subsidy.
- Federal government pays difference up to amount per unit it would contribute in conventional public housing program. Hence, this is housing allowance paid to rentor (the housing authority) rather than the occupant, but has limit tied to debt service.
- More flexible than other public housing programs, since it allows use of existing units, scatteration of subsidized families with no "project" atmosphere.
- Includes opportunity for eligible households to locate appropriate existing units, which can then be approved and leased by a local housing authority.

4. *Public Housing Operating Cost Subsidy*
(Brooke Amendment)
- Federal government pays difference between annual operating costs of public housing and 25 percent of tenants' incomes, allowing reduction of rents below actual operating costs so very low-income tenants will not have to pay over 25 percent of their incomes for rent.
- This is housing allowance paid to rentor. It can apply to all three above forms of public housing. In essence, it transforms public housing programs from fixed-limit debt service subsidies into open-ended housing allowances.

Rent Supplements

1. Housing allowance paid to rentor (the owner), who builds new units or rehabilitates old ones and rents to low-income households in special cate-

gories. Federal government pays difference between 25 percent of occupant's income and market rent, but no more than 70 percent of market rent.
2. Eligibility restricted to low-income, low-asset households who are also either displaced by government action, elderly, living in substandard housing, in homes damaged by natural disaster, or on active duty in armed forces.
3. Can be used with Section 236 program to make some units in moderate-income multi-family buildings available to low-income households. Restricted eligibility makes this best for elderly, since it is largest group eligible for rent supplements.

Income Tax Deductibility

1. Saving on federal income tax for homeowners who occupy own homes, since they are allowed to deduct mortgage interest payments and local property taxes from their federally taxable income—but renters are not.
2. True subsidy lies in inconsistent treatment of homeowner-occupants and rental occupants. Homeowner-occupants are allowed to deduct *some* housing expenses (interest and taxes) but not *all* (such as maintenance and depreciation), but do not have to pay tax on "profit" from renting homes to themselves. Owners of rental dwellings can deduct all expenses, but must pay such income taxes. Result is a tax advantage to homeowner-occupants who itemize deductions on federal income tax forms.
3. This subsidy does not appear in federal budget, since it results from tax reductions caused by original terms of income tax laws passed before 1920. It may not have been intended as a housing subsidy by Congress. Nevertheless, its reality as a true subsidy is proven by emphasis upon such tax savings used by promoters of homeownership trying to persuade renters to buy.

Accelerated Depreciation

1. Saving on federal income taxes because of larger depreciation allowances on housing investments during early years of investment than allowed on other types of property. Depreciation allowances can be deducted from property income before computing federal taxes. Hence, making them larger provides tax shelter for high-bracket investors when taxable net income from property is *negative* and can be subtracted from *other* taxable income before computing taxes due.
2. Expenditures for rehabilitation work on low-income housing units can be written off in five years under Section 167K of the Internal Revenue Code.

Section 221 (d)(2)

1. Extended loan coverage on mortgages to reduce down payments on home purchases financed with market rate mortgages to as low as $200. No cash subsidies are provided, but government insures high risk mortgages and thereby assumes higher chance of foreclosure and repossession. The extra costs resulting from higher risks are in fact a subsidy.
2. This program is not included in most of this analysis, but is identified here because it has highest default rates of any current program, and is often confused with Section 235 existing program.

Sections 223 and 237

1. Programs that allow market interest rate loans to be made to persons with poor credit qualifications, or living in relatively high risk neighborhoods. As in 221 (d)(2), true subsidy lies in likely high foreclosure and repossession costs from loans under other programs that would not have been made except for special insurance provided by these two Sections.

Section 221 (d)(3)– (Below Market Interest Rate)

1. Rental housing subsidy for moderate-income households very similar to Section 236 except has fixed interest rate reduction subsidy resulting from use of three percent mortgage loans.
2. Has all other additional subsidies of Section 236 with about same terms.
3. No longer being generated, but still covers many units built under it from 1962 through 1970.

Sections 115 and 312

1. Section 115 allows capital grants of up to $3,500 to low-income households living in urban renewal areas for rehabilitation of housing units they own.
2. Section 312 allows three percent loans for rehabilitation of properties in urban renewal areas, code enforcement areas, or areas likely to become one or the other. This provides an interest rate reduction subsidy.

Section 502

1. Farmers Home Administration homeownership loan program to households living in areas with less than 10,000 population who cannot obtain adequate

credit elsewhere. No statutory income limits, but administered mainly to moderate-income households.

2. Can include interest rate reduction subsidy similar to Section 235, or interest rate reduction subsidy resulting from Farmers Home Administration lending at below market rate because it floats bonds at low rates. Majority of Section 502 loans made at interest rates *below* what Farmers Home Administration pays buyers of its bonds.

3. Can be used to build new, purchase existing, or rehabilitate existing single-family units.

Section 515

1. Rental and cooperative housing program under Farmers Home Administration for low- and moderate-income households. Two versions—one with fixed interest rate reduction subsidy at three percent (like Section 221 (d)(3)), the other with variable interest rate reduction subsidy (like Section 236).

Bibliography

Aaron, Henry J. "Income Taxes and Housing." *American Economic Review*, December 1970, pp. 789–806.

——. *Shelter and Subsidies*. Washington, D.C.: The Brookings Institution, 1972.

Brueggeman, William B., Ronald L. Racster, and Halbert C. Smith. "Research Report: Multiple Housing Programs and Urban Housing Policy." *AIP Journal* 38, 3 (May 1972): 160–67.

Canty, Donald. "Metropolity." *City* 6, 2 (March-April 1972): 29–44.

Cochran, Clay, and George Rucker. "Every American Family Housing Need and Non-Response." *Papers Submitted to Subcommittee on Housing Panels, Part II*. Committee on Banking and Currency, United States House of Representatives, 92nd Congress. Washington, D.C.: U.S. Government Printing Office, June 1971, pp. 525–41.

Committee on Banking and Currency, United States House of Representatives. *Basic Laws and Authorities on Housing and Urban Development* (Revised through January 31, 1971). Washington, D.C.: U.S. Government Printing Office, 1971.

Committee on Banking and Currency, United States Senate. *Report on the Housing and Urban Development Act of 1968*. Washington, D.C.: U.S. Government Printing Office, 1968.

County of Los Angeles Department of Urban Affairs, Housing Development Services. *Survey of HUD 236 Housing Program in Los Angeles County*. Los Angeles, 1972.

Curzan, Myron P. "Housing and the Role of Large Corporate Enterprise." *Papers Submitted to Subcommittee on Housing Panels, Part I*. Committee on Banking and Currency, United States House of Representatives, 92nd Congress. Washington, D.C.: U.S. Government Printing Office, June 1971, pp. 183–203.

de Leeuw, Frank. "The Housing Allowance Approach." *Papers Submitted to Subcommittee on Housing Panels, Part II*. Committee on Banking and Currency, United States House of Representatives, 92nd Congress. Washington, D.C.: U.S. Government Printing Office, June 1971, pp. 541–54.

——. *Income and the Cost of Rental Housing*. Washington, D.C.: The Urban Institute (Working Paper 112-11), January 28, 1970.

—— and Sam H. Leaman. *The Section 23 Leasing Program*. Washington, D.C.: The Urban Institute (Working Paper 716-1), November 24, 1971.

——, Sam H. Leaman, and Helen Blank. *The Design of a Housing Allowance*. Washington, D.C.: The Urban Institute, October 1970.

Downs, Anthony. "Are Subsidies the Best Answer for Housing Low and Moderate Income Households?" *The Urban Lawyer* 4, 3 (Summer 1972): 405–16.

——. *Urban Problems and Prospects*. Chicago: Markham Publishing Company, 1971.

Executive Office of the President. Office of Management and Budget. *The Budget of the United States Government, Fiscal Year 1973*. Washington, D.C.: U.S. Government Printing Office, 1972.

——. *Special Analyses: Budget of the United States Government, Fiscal Year 1972*. Washington, D.C.: U.S. Government Printing Office, 1971.

——. *Special Analyses: Budget of the United States Government, Fiscal Year 1973*. Washington, D.C.: U.S. Government Printing Office, 1972.

Heinberg, John D. *The Transfer Cost of a Housing Allowance: Conceptual Issues and Benefit Patterns*. Washington, D.C.: The Urban Institute, May 1971.

Joint Economic Committee, Congress of the United States, Staff Study. *The Economics of Federal Subsidy Programs*. Washington, D.C.: U.S. Government Printing Office, January 11, 1972.

Lansing, John B., Charles Wade Clifton, and James N. Morgan. *New Homes and Poor People*. Ann Arbor: Institute for Social Research of the University of Michigan, 1969.

Leaman, Sam H. *Estimated Administrative Cost of a National Housing Allowance*. Washington, D.C.: The Urban Institute (Working Paper 112–17), revised February 2, 1971.

Lozano, Eduardo E. "Technical Report: Housing Costs and Alternative Cost Reducing Policies." *AIP Journal* 38, 3 (May 1972): 176–81.

Macey, John. *Publicly Provided and Assisted Housing the U.S.A.* Washington, D.C.: The Urban Institute (Working Paper: 209–1–4), 1972.

Moskof, Howard R. "Foreign Housing Subsidy Systems: Alternative Approaches." *Papers Submitted on Housing Panels, Part II*. Committee on Banking and Currency, United States House of Representatives, 92nd Congress. Washington, D.C.: U.S. Government Printing Office, June 1971, pp. 627–51.

Office of Audit, U.S. Department of Housing and Urban Development. *Audit Review of Section 235 Single Family Housing* (05-22001-4900). Washington, D.C., December 10, 1971.

——. *Report on Audit of Section 236 Multifamily Housing Program* (05–02–2001–5000). Washington, D.C., January 29, 1972.

President of the United States. *First Annual Report on National Housing Goals*. Washington, D.C.: U.S. Government Printing Office, 1969.

——. *Second Annual Report on National Housing Goals*. Washington, D.C.: U.S. Government Printing Office, 1970.

——. *Third Annual Report on National Housing Goals*. Washington, D.C.: U.S. Government Printing Office, 1971.

——. *Fourth Annual Report on National Housing Goals*. Washington, D.C.: U.S. Government Printing Office, 1972.

The President's Committee on Urban Housing. *A Decent Home*. Washington, D.C.: U.S. Government Printing Office, 1969.

——. *Technical Studies. Volume I: Housing Needs, Federal Housing Programs*. Washington, D.C.: U.S. Government Printing Office, 1967.

Schechter, Henry B., and Marion K. Schlefer. "Housing Needs and National Goals." *Papers Submitted to Subcommittee on Housing Panels, Part I*. Committee on Banking and Currency, United States House of Representatives, 92nd Congress. Washington, D.C..: U.S. Government Printing Office, June 1971, pp. 1–140.

Schultze, Charles L., Edward R. Fried, Alice M. Rivlin, and Nancy H. Teeters. *Setting National Priorities: The 1972 Budget.* Washington, D.C.: The Brookings Institution, 1971.

———. *Setting National Priorities: The 1973 Budget.* Washington, D.C.: The Brookings Institution, 1972.

Secretary of Housing and Urban Development. Letter to Chairman, Committee on Banking, Housing, and Urban Affairs, United States Senate, on defaults and foreclosures among HUD-assisted mortgages. Read into the Congressional Record - Senate, February 8, 1972.

———. Statement before the Subcommittee on Housing of the Committee on Banking and Currency, United States House of Representatives, on settlement costs, mortgage foreclosure, housing abandonment, and site selection policies, February 22, 1972.

———.Statement before the Legal and Monetary Affairs Subcommittee of the Committee on Government Operations, United States House of Representatives, on the operation of the Federal Housing Administration, May 3, 1972.

Shipp, Royal. "Evaluation of Federal Housing Programs: Progress and Prospects." *Proceedings: American Real Estate and Urban Economics Association, Volume V: 1970.* American Real Estate and Urban Economics Association, March 1971.

Subcommittee of the Committee on Appropriations, United States House of Representatives, 92nd Congress, First Session. *HUD-Space-Science Appropriations for 1972: Hearings, Part 3, Department of Housing and Urban Development.* Washington, D.C.: U.S. Government Printing Office, 1971.

Subcommittee on HUD-Space-Science-Veterans, Committee on Appropriations, United States House of Representatives, 92nd Congress, Second Session. *HUD-Space-Science-Veterans Appropriations for 1973: Hearings, Part 3, Budget Amendments, Department of Housing and Urban Development.* Washington, D.C.: U.S. Government Printing Office, 1972.

United States Bureau of the Census. *Demographic, Economic and Revenue Trends for Major Central Cities.* Prepared for a September 9, 1971 meeting with Secretary Romney, Washington, D.C.

———. "Poverty Increases by 1.2 Million in 1970." *Current Population Reports: Consumer Income.* Series P–60, No. 77, May 7, 1971.

United States Department of Housing and Urban Development. *HUD Statistical Yearbook: 1966, 1967, 1968, 1969, 1970.* Washington, D.C.: U.S. Government Printing Office, 1967, 1968, 1969, 1970, 1971.

———. *Justification for 1973 Estimates: Part 2 — Housing Production and Mortgage Credit.* Prepared for the Committee on Appropriations, United States House of Representatives, February 1972.

———. *Justification for 1973 Estimates: Part 3—Housing Management.* Prepared for the Committee on Appropriations, United States House of Representatives, February 1972.

United States House of Representatives, 90th Congress, Second Session. *Conference Report on the Housing and Urban Development Act of 1968* (Report

No. 1785). Washington, D.C.: U.S. Government Printing Office, 1968.
United States National Commission on Urban Problems. *Building the American City*. 91st United States Congress, First Session.
Welfeld, Irving H. "That 'Housing Problem'—the American vs. the European Experience." *The Public Interest*, Spring 1972, pp. 78–95.
——. "Toward a New Federal Housing Policy." *The Public Interest*, Spring 1970, pp. 31–43.

Index

About the Author

Anthony Downs, chairman of the board of Real Estate Research Corporation, is a consultant on urban affairs, government organization, and land use economics. His long-term experience in analyzing low- and moderate-income housing problems includes preparation of several chapters of the *Report of the National Advisory Commission on Civil Disorders*; membership on the President's National Commission on Urban Problems; statistical analysis and evaluation published as *Who Are the Urban Poor?*; many assignments for the U.S. Department of Housing and Urban Development; and preparation of the chapter, "Moving Toward Realistic Housing Goals," for the Brookings Institution's *Agenda for the Nation.* Dr. Downs is the author of *An Economic Theory of Democracy, Inside Bureaucracy,* and *Urban Problems and Prospects.* He is coauthor of *Achieving Effective Desegregation: A Handbook,* also published by Lexington Books.